WRITERS AND THEIR WORK

ISOBEL ARMSTRONG
*General Editor*

BRYAN LOUGHREY
*Advisory Editor*



# PAUL SCOTT

*The British Council*

PAUL SCOTT

# PAUL SCOTT

Jacqueline Banerjee

NORTHCOTE

BRITISH COUNCIL

ATLANTIC
PUBLISHERS & DISTRIBUTORS (P) LTD

This edition is published by

**ATLANTIC**

PUBLISHERS & DISTRIBUTORS (P) LTD

7/22, Ansari Road, Darya Ganj, New Delhi-110 002
Tel: 40775252, 23273880, 23275880, 23280451; Fax: +91-11-23285873
E-mail: orders@atlanticbooks.com; Web: www.atlanticbooks.com

By arrangement with
**Northcote House Publishers Ltd**
Horndon House, Horndon, Tavistock, Devon, PL19 9NQ,
United Kingdom. (T)+44(0)1822 810066; (F)+44(0)1822 810034
(E) northcote.house@virgin.net and (W) www.northcotehouse.co.uk
The *Writers and their Work* series is published in association with
the British Council.


**First Indian Reprint 2010**
First published in 1999 by Northcote House Publishers Ltd

ISBN 978-81-269-1292-6



**British Library Cataloguing-in-Publication Data**
A catalogue record for this book is available from the British Library

Typeset by PDQ Typesetting, Newcastle-under-Lyme
Printed in India at Nice Printing Press, A-33/3A, Site-IV,
Industrial Area, Sahibabad, Ghaziabad, U.P.

For my family in India,
with affection and respect

# Contents

# Biographical Outline

| | |
|---|---|
| 1920 | Paul Mark Scott born 25 March to Tom Scott and Frances (née Mark), in Southgate, north London. |
| 1929 | Enters the Winchmore Hill Collegiate School. |
| c. 1934/5 | Withdrawn from school; taken on as accountant's boy by C. T. Payne in Regent Street. |
| 1940 | Enlists as a private in the 8th Battalion, the Buffs. Posted to Torquay. Poetic trilogy, *I Gerontius*, published. |
| 1941 | Marries Nancy Edith Avery (Penny). |
| 1942 | Poems published in *Poetry Quarterly* and the anthology *Poets of This War*. |
| 1943 | Posted to India and sent to the Officers' Training School at Belgaum in western India. Commissioned into the Royal Indian Army Service Corps. |
| 1944 | Sent to Assam as second-in-command of a section of No. 1 Indian Air Supply Command. Promoted to Captain. Accompanies some flights into Burma. |
| 1945 | Posted to Malaya for mopping-up operations. |
| 1946 | Demobilized in Deolali after sixth months in Bihar. Appointed bookkeeper to Falcon and Grey Walls Press, rising to Company Secretary. |
| 1947 | Birth of first daughter, Carol Vivien. |
| 1948 | *Pillars of Salt* published as one of *Four Jewish Plays*. Birth of second daughter, Sally Elizabeth. |
| 1950 | Becomes a literary agent with Pearn, Pollinger and Higham. |
| 1952 | Radio play, *Lines of Communication*, broadcast and subsequently adapted for television. First novel, *Johnnie Sahib*, wins the Eyre and Spottiswoode Literary Award. |

| | |
|---|---|
| 1953 | *The Alien Sky* published. |
| 1954 | Appointed to directorship at Pearn, Pollinger and Higham. Radio adaptation of *The Alien Sky*. |
| 1956 | Television adaptation of *The Alien Sky*. *A Male Child* published. |
| 1958 | *The Mark of the Warrior* published. Radio play *Sahibs and Memsahibs* broadcast. Death of Tom Scott; breach with Frances Scott. |
| 1959 | First of several visits to the Costa Brava. Radio adaptation of *The Mark of the Warrior*. |
| 1960 | *The Chinese Love Pavilion* published. Resigns from Higham's. |
| 1962 | *The Birds of Paradise* published. |
| 1963 | Elected Fellow of the Royal Society of Literature. *The Bender* published. Travels to the US for the American launch. |
| 1964 | *The Corrida at San Feliu* published. First return visit to India. Television adaptation of *The Bender*. |
| 1966 | *The Jewel in the Crown* published. |
| 1968 | *The Day of the Scorpion* published. |
| 1969 | *The Towers of Silence* published. Another visit to India. |
| 1972 | British Council lecture tour in India. |
| 1974 | *A Division of the Spoils* published. |
| 1975 | Lecture trip to America, speaking at campuses in Texas, Washington, Maryland and Illinois. |
| 1976 | *Staying On* published. Penny starts legal proceedings to end the marriage. Visiting Professorship for the fall semester at the University of Tulsa in Oklahoma. |
| 1977 | Travels to the US for the American launch of *Staying On* and a summer school programme in Detroit. Operated on for colon cancer on his visit to Tulsa. *Staying On* is awarded the Booker Prize. Reunited with Penny on return to England. |
| 1978 | Dies in the Middlesex Hospital, London, on 1 March, after a second operation for cancer. |

# Abbreviations and References

Editions of Paul Scott's works used in this study:

| | |
|---|---|
| *PS* | *Pillars of Salt* (in *Four Jewish Plays*, Victor Gollancz, 1948) |
| *JS* | *Johnnie Sahib* (Panther, 1979) |
| *AS* | *The Alien Sky* (Heinemann, 1978) |
| *MW* | *The Mark of the Warrior* (Heinemann, 1978) |
| *CLP* | *The Chinese Love Pavilion* (Heinemann, 1978) |
| *BP* | *The Birds of Paradise* (Eyre and Spottiswoode, 1960) |
| *B* | *The Bender* (Panther, 1975) |
| *CSF* | *The Corrida at San Feliu* (Secker and Warburg, 1964) |
| *JC* | *The Jewel in the Crown* (Mandarin, 1996) |
| *DSc* | *The Day of the Scorpion* (Mandarin, 1996) |
| *TS* | *The Towers of Silence* (Mandarin, 1996) |
| *DSp* | *A Division of the Spoils* (Mandarin, 1996) |
| *SO* | *Staying On* (Mandarin, 1996) |
| *AF* | *After the Funeral* (Whittington Press and Heinemann, 1979) |
| *MAM* | *My Appointment with the Muse: Essays, 1961–75*, edited by Shelley C. Reece (Heinemann, 1986) |

# Introduction

Paul Scott's obituary in *The Times* of 3 March 1978 carried the heading 'Author of "The Raj Quartet"', and that is how he continues to be known. The distinction, however, has had its disadvantages. The four hefty inter-related novels, issued in a one-volume edition in 1976, have tended to be seen as an account of times past in a distant country, coming at the tail-end of the Kipling/Forster tradition. This, moreover, was in an age when Indian writing in English was already flourishing. For example, before the *Quartet* was even completed, some of the historical events towards which it moves, such as the horrors of Partition and the decline of the princely states, had themselves already been the subject of such compelling Indian novels as Kushwant Singh's *Train to Pakistan* (1956) and Manohar Malgonkar's *The Princes* (1963). Commonwealth Literature courses in the universities naturally focused on such works, and the recent replacement of those courses with the Postcolonial Literature speciality did not produce any immediate surge of interest in authors writing 'from the outside'.

On the contrary, the new academic label, with its implication of a successful emergence from colonial oppression, particularly favoured radical texts which documented the progress towards such an emergence, and/or helped to establish a new reading of the ex-colonies' history. This is easily understood in the light of the need to right old wrongs, and the even more urgent need to build confidence in the national and cultural identity of the newly liberated countries. As for the peoples who had for so long thwarted this process, there could be little interest in re-examining *their* roles, or in analysing the effects of the colonial past upon *them*.

Yet these were just the kind of issues with which Paul Scott was concerned. He felt strongly that 'the ignorance of India of a vast majority of British living on their own island' was something to be 'taken account of', something to be addressed. This was not a matter of introducing 'Indian manners, customs, religious and domestic arrangements' to them; it was a matter of making a new honest assessment of (for example) 'the multiple and conflicting interests that were at stake' during the last days of empire, and 'the many-faceted response of individual Indians to individual Britons and vice-versa' (*MAM* 121). This, to my mind, is exactly what he achieves in the *Raj Quartet*.

However, a work which challenges as simplistic the 'picture of a tyrannical and imperialistic power grinding the faces of its coloured subjects in the dust' (*JC* 381) was bound not only to be ignored by academe, but also to attract the wrath of those still engaged in settling old scores. On 29 March 1984, Christopher Morahan, the producer and co-director of *The Jewel in the Crown* (the title given to the television serialization of the *Quartet*), wrote indignantly to the editor of the *Listener* about the previous week's selection of quotations from a 'Did You See . . . ?' programme on the serial. ' . . . in no way could this programme be interpreted as anything other than a knocking job', he complained, adding that the selection itself had compounded this effect. In January 1985, Salman Rushdie added considerable weight to the attack when he wrote a short but influential piece in the periodical *American Film*, condemning what he saw as an upsurge of nostalgia for the Raj on British television, and dismissing *The Jewel in the Crown* in his opening paragraph as 'grotesquely overpraised'. Rushdie went further. Later in his article, he found an opportunity to criticize Scott's literary judgement (in his capacity as the literary agent of M. M. Kaye, author of *The Far Pavilions*, 1977), and he then suggested that as a novelist Scott was nothing but a pale copy of E. M. Forster. Worst of all, he claimed that Scott reinforces old stereotypes ('white society's fear of the darkie') by using the gang-rape of a British girl in India, by Indian peasants, as a central motif for his whole long work.[1]

Commercial decisions and ventures have to be made with commercial ends in view, and the widespread success of both *The Far Pavilions* and the television adaptation of the *Raj Quartet* provides one answer to Rushdie's earlier complaints. As for the more damaging and crucial parts of Rushdie's attack, which seem to be aimed at the literary work itself, they represent hasty judgements which are not at all borne out by a careful reading of it. The rape of Daphne Manners in the Bibighar Gardens will be considered in detail in Chapter 4. Suffice it to say here quite categorically that, far from reinforcing prejudice, Scott uses all the means at his disposal – historical as well as novelistic – to undermine and destroy it. Among the most important points Scott makes are that Daphne's attackers *inside* the Gardens are never identified (she herself is prepared to testify that they could have been British), and that those who attack her just as hurtfully *outside* the Gardens are definitely British. The fact that Daphne's fellow victim in all this is an innocent Indian also works strongly to disturb old stereotypes, reminding the reader that the rape itself is an ironic inversion of the rape of India by the British.

But it has to be admitted that Scott was taking big risks here. He was catching on the raw the sensibilities of those who had so recently freed themselves from their colonial fetters; and he was endangering his own reputation into the bargain. For it is only within the last few years that the theoretical base of post-colonialism has been broadened to admit the growing body of writing which, like his, refuses to sit neatly on one side of the racial divide. It has taken a decade and more for weight to be given to the more precise, chronological meaning of the prefix 'post'. Perhaps Neil Lazarus, in a discussion of postcolonial African fiction in 1990, was the first to notice how 'reductive' the *anti*colonial enterprise was becoming. Lazarus realized, for example, how 'radical anticolonial writers tended to romanticize the resistance movement and to underestimate –even theoretically to suppress – the dissensions within it'.[2] More recently, and more importantly for Scott himself, Michael Gorra has argued in a study of Scott, V. S. Naipaul and Rushdie (published in 1997), that while 'a postcolonial literature, a postcolonial politics, inevitably rests on and requires a foundation of anticolonialism . . . it cannot, at the end of the century, be limited to that'. The feeling that there should now be room for works which neither 'attack nor . . . defend', but explore past conflicts and trace their effects into the present, has led Gorra himself to examine Scott's writings alongside those of other, much more obvious candidates for inclusion in the postcolonial category. This move has finally produced the kind of recognition which the *Raj Quartet* had never previously been accorded – as 'the greatest work of fiction that the British produced about their empire'.[3]

Even this, however, may be seen as a kind of marginalization. For it depends on the 'placing' of Scott within the currently fashionable postcolonial debate; and after all, Scott *was* British, and he was shaped by and working within a long heritage to which his own work should be seen as contributing. Moreover, Scott, who saw himself as a writer to whom 'images come first' (*MAM* 54), was adamant that he found the twilight of the Raj less important as a subject in itself than as material which was peculiarly suited to expressing his own artistic vision. In 1972, looking back over his career to date, he told audiences on his British Council tour of India,

> my proper answer to the question, 'Why do you – as a modern English novelist of serious pretensions bother to write about the time-expired subject of the British Raj?' (and that is what is implied) – is, must be, if my novels are novels at all, 'Because the last days of the British Raj are the metaphor I have presently chosen to illustrate my view of life'. (*MAM* 115)

What Scott found in this particular historical upheaval was, fundamentally, a way of confronting the feeling of dispossession which he shared with so many of those contemporaries whose very ignorance of India he deplored. Of course, the break-up of empire, in itself, contributed greatly to this feeling; but it went much deeper than that. Scott's ambivalence about his art ('if my novels are novels at all'), confirms that he was writing very much within the larger cultural climate of his times. It was a period in which the sense of fragmentation expressed by the modernists was giving rise to radical questioning of the nature and role of fiction – the kind of questioning which informed Scott's own lectures during the later sixties and seventies.[4] Indeed, it proved to be especially fruitful in Scott's case, bringing him to see the novel not as a vehicle of '*definitive* experience' (*MAM* 84), but as an 'area of creative contact between two people' (*MAM* 89). It does Scott less than justice, then, to see him as chronicling, however well, and on whatever scale, a specific era in a specific country.

Ironically, though, in the eyes of the growing number of scholars who have taken up Scott's work, and of the general public, the *Raj Quartet* does completely overshadow Scott's earlier writings. Even his most sympathetic critics use the eight preceding novels largely as hunting-grounds for character-types and themes which, they suggest, are more fully developed in the *Quartet*, or for signs of that technical expertise which (they also suggest) finally flowers in his masterpiece. In K. Bhaskara Rao's *Paul Scott* (1980), for instance, some of Scott's best work is discussed under the chapter heading 'Pointing to the Raj Quartet'.

But the word 'presently' which Scott used in the speech quoted above is a reminder that he used other metaphors, too, to express his artistic vision. Another reason his earlier work has been neglected (besides the emphasis laid on the *Raj Quartet*) is that these metaphors have been less appealing both to academics and to the reading public. Until quite recently, they have been largely to the side of what is fashionable in contemporary literature: in representing and grappling with the problems of cultural and personal identity, Scott was particularly concerned with the male role. The heroes of his first eight novels are deployed in a variety of situations: they work in army depots, rehearse for jungle warfare, suffer as POWs, dig the parched soil, pour out their souls to strangers at the bar, and so forth. Through such situations, Scott explores the various contradictory demands among which men have to negotiate – to act according to ideals, for instance, without sacrificing their individuality or their hold on reality; or to protect freedom and yet forge bonds. The last days of the Raj also provided a compelling metaphor for Scott because here the older fiction of proud male dominance with all its obligations (duty, responsibility and so forth) had been so powerfully challenged by a newer one (involving sensitivity to others, an acceptance of their autonomy, and a willingness to make new kinds of commitments to them) in a real-life drama of almost mythic dimensions.

Scott's choice of metaphors was by no means random, then, and he liked to see himself as 'a social novelist' (*MAM* 127); on the other hand he knew that 'Writing a novel is like peeling an onion' and that he was revealing in his work aspects of himself that could not be expressed in his daily life (*MAM* 141). Chief among these was his anxiety about what one psychologist working in the area of male identity has termed 'handicap at love'.[5] For Scott found that he could not live with the dispossessed, fragmented self. On the contrary, restructuring it became the central and fundamental concern of his work, and one in which he successfully involves his readers. Of post-modern tendencies, this indeed puts him most in line with the postcolonial. But the plight of the brown Englishman of the *Raj Quartet*, Harry Coomer, does not simply mirror that of new generations of people who find themselves in a whole new cultural situation, either in their own country or amid the ethnic diversity of a newly multicultural Britain. It also and more fundamentally mirrors that of Scott himself, for whom class, profession and even sexuality would all turn out to be areas of conflict. That is why, in the end, the process of restructuring the identity is one into which matters of race and gender, along with the particulars of place, era and historical change, are all subsumed. By clarifying Scott's aims and vision as a novelist, this study seeks to re-evaluate his earlier work, as well as to strengthen the claims of the *Raj Quartet* to be considered one of the major works of twentieth-century (not just postcolonial) literature.

# 1

# A Divided Life

Paul Scott was born on 25 March 1920, not in some exotic outpost of empire but in the front bedroom of a rented semi-detached house in the north London borough of Southgate. There was a sense of dispossession from the start, or at least there were some unfortunate comparisons to be made: his father, Tom Scott, was a commercial artist who could recall his family's heyday in the north, and whose studio was less successful than that of his cousins, the Wrights, who catered for more upmarket clients in Richmond. Paul and his elder brother Peter were sent to the Winchmore Hill Collegiate, a private school with a good local reputation, but Paul nevertheless felt and minded the economic strain under which the household operated. In *The Bender* (1963), he writes about a father who 'painted pictures for Christmas cards, chocolate box covers and calendars' and tried 'to maintain the standards of a gentleman even in a suburban, terraced villa', but was generally 'much in arrears' with his second son's school fees (p. 20). Here, then, was someone well equipped to appreciate the struggles of ex-colonials to hold on to their dignity under post-independence conditions in India.

Visits to the two family studios did more than make Scott sensitive to economic pressures: they led to his boyhood hobby of producing, with his brother, amateur films drawn in Indian ink and passed through ingenious home-made projectors. The slow, painstaking process trained him to work patiently towards long-term goals; it also directly encouraged the literary aspirations inherited from his mother Frances, a woman from a working-class background who had burned her unpublished novels the night before her wedding.[1] By the age of 9, Scott was inventing plots and dialogue for characters modelled on the cinema stars of the day. From here it was an easy step to discovering 'the power of words without pictures' (*MAM* 154), although verbal images would always provide essential starting points for his writing, and punctuate his narratives.

However, it would be many years before he could enjoy the luxury of becoming a full-time writer. Tom Scott lost his precarious foothold in residential Southgate during the Depression, and temporarily moved the family in with his two unmarried sisters on Southgate High Street. A period of tension followed between the elderly aunts who were set in their ways, and Scott's young and volatile mother – uncomfortable enough at the time, though all grist to the mill when he came to explore women in families like the Hursts in *A Male Child* (1956) and the Laytons in the *Raj Quartet*. Then, worse still, he was prematurely withdrawn from school and set to work as an accountant's boy in C. T. Payne's small office in Regent Street. In *The Bender*, Tim Spruce also has to leave school at 16 and become an accountant. Later, an elderly partner in the firm recalls 'the pretentious mother who had come to speak up for him at his interview', and the behind-the-scenes laughter which this had occasioned (p. 105). The reference to the mother is telling; Scott's humiliation must have been complete.

Interestingly, however, the feeling of disappointment in *The Bender* is deflected from the accountant Tim on to his younger brother George, because George has *failed* to find a steady occupation, however humdrum. In a translation of Stendhal's *Souvenirs d'Egotisme*, George comes across the words, 'Without work the vessel of life has no ballast' (p. 17), and at once recognizes his own problem. Scott himself knuckled down to his work with characteristic seriousness, and took satisfaction from his successes in his professional exams. Eventually he was to look back on his office life with pride rather than bitterness: 'I was, if you will allow me to say so, a very good bookkeeper' (*MAM* 160).

Still, he knew the books he was sitting in front of were 'the wrong sort of books' for him (*CSF* 22), and from now on, Scott's was very much a divided life: in time snatched from his accountancy studies, he embarked on a literary apprenticeship as well, first with the encouragement of one of Payne's clients (who appears to have influenced him at least as much by his homosexuality as by introducing him to the works of Oscar Wilde), and then under the tutelage of a poet and schoolteacher who happened to be living next door to the Scotts at that time.[2] Talking to the London Writer Circle many years later as their President, in an address which he described as 'the autobiography of *the writer* in me', Scott spoke with gratitude of the guidance he received during this period, and recalled vividly the opening up of his literary horizons. Among the 'pantheon of modern literary gods' which he discovered, he listed W. H. Auden, T. S. Eliot, Christopher Isherwood, Henrik Ibsen and Anton Chekhov; and he spoke also of 'renewing acquaintance' with some earlier favourites, like Sir Walter Scott (*MAM* 152, 155). In another address of the same 'meet the author' variety (in fact, that was the title of the speech), he mentioned reading Ralph Waldo Emerson in his youth as well, and while a number of Emerson's essays are quoted in his later writings, on that occasion he singled out for particular comment the essay on 'History' (*MAM* 47).

The mix here is both fascinating and deeply relevant to Scott's future career as a writer. The modernist poets, for instance, would have sharpened his awareness of the cultural and spiritual dilemmas of the time, and his own feeling of alienation – 'the feeling that you are somehow separate from your environment and can't identify with it really satisfactorily' (*MAM* 4). The impact of *The Waste Land*, in particular, is all too clear from his first published work, *I, Gerontius* (1940), a verse trilogy as overblown as it is derivative. But the unmistakably genuine *cri de coeur* with which this poem ends, a prayer for the preservation of the 'Peoples of the Earth' ('Requiem'), points forward to a time when Eliot's influence on him would be at once more diffuse and more positive. In later years, it would emanate more from the spiritual discoveries of *Four Quartets* than from the overwhelming impression of spiritual sterility in *The Waste Land*; Scott was to give full credit to this source of inspiration, but not without pointing out that 'no one exerts an influence unless there is already a correspondence of outlook for the influence to work upon' (*MAM* 119).

There could have been few would-be writers of those years who did not come under Eliot's sway. Scott's interest in Ibsen and Chekhov comes as no surprise either, in view of his early experiments in drama. More noteworthy are the two threads which run through Scott's other early reading – the homosexual (Wilde, Auden and Isherwood); and the historical (Walter Scott, and Emerson's 'History'). As yet, Scott confessed wryly in his speech to the London Writer Circle, 'the world of the novel seemed too vast and laborious' to him (*MAM* 155), and when he did try to write one, he soon ran out of steam. But there was much here that would feed productively into his later work, not least perhaps from Isherwood's writings of this period, the novel *Mr Norris Changes Trains* (1935) and the sketches in *Goodbye to Berlin* (1939). These were both to have been part of a larger project which never materialized, and deal with the overlapping experiences of people living in Berlin at a time of great social upheaval. There were clues here not only for Scott's future subject matter (in which India, with all its vastness and complexity, would replace Berlin), but also for its treatment. Isherwood's words at the beginning of *Goodbye to Berlin* ('I am a camera . . .') would also have provided a corrective to Scott's literary namesake's romanticism – though it is worth remembering, too, how important Sir Walter Scott himself was to the realist project of the Victorian novelists.

By the time he was called up for active service in the Second World War, then, Scott had a gone through a useful programme of reading, had several short manuscripts in hand (he would speak amusingly, later, of his first rejections), and was beginning to recognize his own authentic voice (*MAM* 155–7). Clearly, it was not the war which made him a writer; however, it did give him the inspiration he was looking for.

The first major changes in his life came before his posting to India: while he was at training camp in Torquay as a private with the 8th Battalion, the Buffs, both his Southgate aunts were killed in an air raid, and after a period of confusion and loneliness which worried his friends at home, he met and married Nancy Avery (Penny), a young Ward Sister from the Rosehill Children's Hospital, Torquay. His delight in Penny's more outgoing, less complicated personality, and her devotion to him, made this marriage one of the mainstays of his life. Yet it may not have been quite the typical wartime romance that it seems. There is mounting evidence that some of Scott's earlier confusion had been over his sexual identity. The marriage might therefore have been as much a deliberate assertion of choice as his earlier decision to keep up with his literary efforts; but what was asserted now was perhaps not so much his deepest impulse, as the need to conform.[3] This time it would not have been simply a matter of juggling two separate calls on his time, but of repressing a part of himself which would not emerge again except in his fiction, in the kind of denial embodied in characters like the 'fairy' Sanderson in *The Alien Sky* (1953) with his 'high-pitched and effeminate' voice (p. 56) or, more honestly and powerfully, in troubled figures like Major Reid in *The Chinese Love Pavilion* (1960) and Ronald Merrick in the *Raj Quartet*. Obviously, this might help to explain Scott's difficulty in expressing his feelings, his uncertainty about the male role, and the kinds of relationships which his male characters establish with each other – and with women. Less obviously, it might also explain his interest in characters like Dorothy Gower in *The Alien Sky*, whose personality has been inhibited and even warped by the effort to keep her Eurasian origins a secret.

At any rate, by the time he sailed for India in the spring of 1943, Scott had seen *I, Gerontius* in print in a shilling broadsheet, had had a few poems published in *Poetry Quarterly* and Patricia Ledward and Colin Strang's anthology *Poems of this War* (1942); and he had a wife. Of the two pieces in the anthology, 'Time' shows him dealing with 'young sweet love', while 'Death of a Hero' adds to this natural preoccupation an equally natural anxiety about the risk of a lonely death in war: 'And you will not be there (and this last pain/ Will hurt him most . . . will rend his heart again)'. Both use conventional vocabulary, with the latter, in particular, echoing earlier war poetry: to borrow a comment made in *A Male Child*, 'All the sonnets are derivative of course. He had a Rupert Brooke period' (p. 197). Yet if there were still no fruits of the more productive reading of the pre-war years, there are hints here of several of Scott's gifts – in 'Time', of his ability to change focus, to set the intimate moment in the larger sweep of place and memory; in 'Death of a Hero', of the dramatic sense he had been developing for years now, and also of the sensitivity to accumulated human suffering which marked his emotional maturity.

This makes it all the more tempting to claim that Scott was ready for India; but he was still very young (only 23) and he was dismayed by his posting, and then again by the hostility of the weather when he disembarked from the Athlone Castle in Bombay in June 1943, during the monsoon. Later, he would talk about the 'shocking ambience of India encountered for the first time' (*MAM* 100). However, like Bob Ramsay in *The Mark of the Warrior* (1958), he soon found this initial shock giving way to 'a sense of discovery' and an acceptance of the need for 'reassessment'; and while 'The picture unfolded further', there was the challenge that presented itself the moment he arrived at the Officer's Training Camp at Belgaum, in the Western Ghats – that of doing a job of work, however uncongenial (*MW* 19–21). Thus was born what Scott was to call 'a double obsession' in his novels: 'an obsession with British India and an obsession with the importance to the main characters of their work' (*MAM* 117).

In retrospect, it does seem fitting that Scott should have arrived in India at that particular point in its history. The Indian Congress Party had been reluctant for the country to be pulled into yet another war, and had taken the opportunity to bargain for independence in return for the much-needed cooperation. When few concessions were forthcoming, Mahatma Gandhi embarked on a new Civil Disobedience campaign, which continued even beyond the fall of Rangoon to the Japanese in March 1942. Mohammed Ali Jinnah and his powerful Muslim League were equally opposed to cooperation with the British, but could not endorse the demands of the Hindu Congress Party for a homogenous nation either. Without Jinnah's support, Congress was unable to hold out against the Raj government, which reacted to the Quit India resolution of 8 August 1942 (less than a year before Scott set foot in Bombay) by declaring the Party illegal and taking stern repressive measures. Over 2,500 civilians had been killed or injured and over 60,000 arrested by the end of the year.[4] Gandhi himself was not released from prison until May 1943, just before Scott's disembarkation. Another thread in the alarming pattern of opposition to the British was the formation of the Indian National Party in Singapore by Subhas Chandra Bose, who had escaped from India in 1941, and whose soldiers advanced with the Japanese in 1943 up to the very border of India. In short, Scott was in India during the final great push for independence, a period of high drama and private suffering for countless Indians and also for the thousands of British who still saw India as their home and its government their duty.

While Scott's own family background made it natural for him to sympathize with people working because they felt they had to, and then clinging desperately to a disappearing lifestyle, his feelings were, as usual, mixed. Looking back in the late sixties, he told the Commonwealth Countries' League in London:

> I'm not at all sure that what cultural shock I suffered wasn't the shock of *Anglo*-India. The people weren't really my sort of people . . . But after I'd become used to it . . . India itself, the country and its people, nudged its way into my affection, and stayed there. (*MAM* 97)

And perhaps this was inevitable, too. Despite the official stances of the Congress Party and the Muslim League, voluntary recruitment in India eventually resulted in over two million Indians (from officers like Sayed Kasim in the *Raj Quartet* to ordinary sepoys) joining the war effort. The princes, advised by British 'Residents' like Sir Robert Conway in *The Birds of Paradise* (1962), and relying on the British to protect their autonomy in the future, also remained loyal. Once he was commissioned into the Royal Indian Army Service Corps, Scott not only experienced life at popular hill stations like Abbottabad (near Kakul, his next training camp after Belgaum) and Murree in the Punjab (where he went after that),[5] but also developed close friendships with his Indian comrades.

Thus, despite his disclaimer at the beginning of *Johnnie Sahib* (1952), that 'The characters in this novel are all imaginary', Scott paints affectionate portraits in it of two Indian havildars (sergeants) serving in his unit of the Indian Air Supply Company. One is the good-natured Nimu, caught surreptitiously teaching an orderly to read; the other is the loyal Dass, who is so deeply relieved when his 'sahib' returns to his section from Marapore. Their names have not even been changed. As for the princes, they were distant figures, but Scott's fascination with them is clear from both *The Birds of Paradise* and *A Division of the Spoils* (1974), and he was distressed by their 'betrayal' when the British left India without safeguarding their traditional rights (*MAM* 19).

Scott's relationship with all his men, including the Indians under his command, was very important to him at the time, and for his fiction later. Typically, his feelings were not uncomplicated. On the simplest level, his concern for them helped him to understand the paternalism, the *man-bap* or mother–father relationship, of the rulers and the ruled in India. In *Johnnie Sahib*, Johnnie sentimentally insists that 'My blokes *belong* to me' (p. 101). There was a certain mystique about it. But there was the responsibility, too, and this had its disturbing side: the wartime leader is, after all, turning those who follow him, as well as himself, into part of the killing machine. As Major Craig, a 'decent, unspectacular man' in *The Mark of the Warrior*, comes to realize with increasing distress, effective leadership involves a loss of humanity (p. 28). The potential for sadism which Scott began to explore in this novel would issue forth again in *The Corrida at San Feliu* (1964), where a matador is seen from a bull's point of view: 'What horned animal had he truly encountered?' (p. 278); and then again, with a vengeance, not only in Ronald Merrick but in many dramatic episodes in the *Raj Quartet*. Events at the end of British rule in India allowed him to express his deepest compulsions as well as anxieties in an indirect, 'metaphorical' way.

Following the fall of Rangoon at the beginning of May 1945, and a period of leave spent savouring the social and cultural life of Calcutta and relaxing on a houseboat in Kashmir, Scott was posted to Malaya. His section was detailed to support the routing of the Japanese, but in the event, the Japanese had already surrendered before they arrived; what Scott endured chiefly during the next few months was only another bout of culture shock. This one, however, was more revealing than the last, for he found himself missing not England but India. As Brian Saxby explains when Tom Brent, the young hero of *The Chinese Love Pavilion*, asks him why India is so important to him:

> Does one acre please you as much as another? Don't you carry in your mind's eye a kind of perfection of landscape your actual eye is always searching to match? . . . Find it, come close to it, there'll be no other quite to come up to it. And your mind's eye being what it is it's just as likely you'll preconceive its whereabouts as not. That's why. That's why India for you. (p. 47)

On the one hand, here is Scott's acceptance of another kind of division in himself, a division of loyalty between two countries; on the other hand, Saxby's reference to the 'mind's eye' recalls what a maharajah has to say about his own small piece of India in *The Alien Sky*, 'Spiritually of course it might be anywhere' (p. 140).

On New Year's Eve, 1945, Scott rejoined the rest of his company in a transit camp near Bihar, and had several months to reflect on his Indian experience before embarking for England in May. It was not just a time for thinking about the past. Although he would miss the final act of the great drama of independence, and the consequent bloodbath of the partition, he was there during some of the crucial episodes that led up to them. Early in 1946 (after the defeat of the Japanese), Bose surrendered and the Indian National Army trials were held in Delhi, rousing the people to a new wave of open rebellion; and in March, Clement Attlee's new Labour government sent out an abortive Cabinet mission to confer with the leaders of the Muslim League and the Congress about the future government of the country. Both these events feature in the brilliant sequence of Halki cartoons in *A Division of the Spoils* (pp. 502–12), invented by Scott as a means of conveying history 'WITHOUT APPEARING TO' (*MAM* 168). When Scott finally embarked for home again after his three years' service there, the country was in a state of high tension. The sense of living in historic times was unavoidable, and for Scott, what was happening in India was not just of local significance:

> India, to me, was the scene of a remarkable and far-reaching event. I see it as the place where the British came to the end of themselves as they were. It was, even more than England was, the scene of the victory of Liberal Humanism over dying paternal imperialism. (*MAM* 48)

Here he himself acknowledges the broadest ideological sense in which India served as a 'metaphor' for his view of life. After more time to absorb and understand this momentous victory, Scott would find it an irresistible subject for his writing; but because of his own first-hand experiences as a leader in India, albeit of a small army unit, he would know better than to present it without its undercurrent of tragedy. As it turned out, this degree of ambivalence would bring him criticism from both sides of the ideological/racial divide, from ex-colonials on the one hand to Rushdie on the other.[6] From a literary perspective, however, their brickbats were to be the inevitable price for creating, out of such emotionally charged material, a narrative in which various points of view are alternately privileged.

Another twenty years would pass, though, before Scott had the confidence and leisure to engage in a vast project like the *Raj Quartet*. First came the urgent need to rehabilitate himself in civilian life in postwar Britain, with a wife and soon two children to support. Attempting to close the gap between his professional career and literary aspirations, he first took up an accountancy job with the Falcon and Grey Walls Press; but before the Press foundered amid scandal, he had the foresight (and integrity) to resign, and in 1950 joined the much more solid and reputable establishment of Pearn, Pollinger and Higham as a literary agent.

By now his own writing career was getting off the ground. One of his early plays, *Pillars of Salt* (1948), had been published as a result of its success in an Anglo-Palestinian play competition. Set 'almost on the border separating two countries' (p. 99), and focusing on the ideological dilemma of two brothers, the play establishes some of the abiding concerns of Scott's *oeuvre*. The editor's introduction, for example, describes it as the work of an author 'strangely affected by the indecency of racial persecution' (n.p.). *Pillars of Salt* is also noteworthy for the appearance in it of a fascist bureaucrat named Stenner. Described in a stage direction as 'tall and well-built... almost military' with 'an arrogance in his face... but... an underlying weakness in him as well' (p. 113), Stenner is 'the eternal superman' who would always fascinate Scott (p. 120), and whose intrusion and highly questionable influence would have to be dealt with all through his work. Here, in a melodramatic ending, the man gets a brutal comeuppance at the hands of the younger of the two brothers, who then escape together to start a new life. More authentic as well as more articulate is *Lines of Communication* (1950), Scott's first postwar work to be accepted – a radio play which draws on his own experiences on the various Indian air-bases. This was also the germ of his first work of prose fiction, *Johnnie Sahib*, publication of which was followed in turn by a television adaptation of the original play. Scott's success with the media, which continued even after his death, is another sign that his writing was very much of its time; however, he had found his form at last – the novel.

Scott's next novel, which again started life as a proposal for a radio play, was the one that really established him. His material here was the very material he would eventually find most compelling and rewarding: *The Alien Sky* is about the British community in an Indian town caught in the build-up of hostilities towards the Raj. Again, there were radio and television adaptations, which showed off to advantage the talents honed from his amateur film-making days; the drama surrounding Dorothy Gower's origins points forward, too. Ironically, it was just at the point of cross-cultural unions like Dorothy's father's that cultural splintering began: 'anything to do with father's second marriage [to Dorothy's Eurasian mother] wasn't recognized by his family' (*AS* 202). Eurasians, of course, were not the only 'social pariahs' treated 'so abominably' by both the British and the Indians (*AS* 36). No fictional character would represent this sad sub-class better than Hari Kumar, brought up in England as Harry Coomer, in the *Raj Quartet*.

Scott's fascination with India fluctuated during the rest of the decade. His third novel, *A Male Child,* deals only with the aftermath of active service in the Far East; the other two highly original works which he completed in the fifties are both set there, but express some ambivalence about it. The treacherous jungles of Burma and India provide the backdrop for *The Mark of the Warrior*, while *The Chinese Love Pavilion* shifts from India to Malaya. In the latter, highly symbolic novel, there are passages of fine (Indian) scene-painting like this:

> On flat endless plains distant and minareted towns glimmered like mirages, and yellow mud-walled villages loomed and were gone, hidden in the dust to crumble away invisibly behind us, forgotten. As the sun fell to the western edge of such plains the violet pigment of its rays would settle low in the air like the lees of wine leaving the sky above us as clear, as pink as sea-shells.

On the other hand, there is some doubt about coping with such vastness: '[it] was a land's land, too vast, too beautiful to harbour well the designs men sought to carve upon it' (*CLP* 50). When

Tom Brent gives up trying to cultivate a strip of land leased from an Indian prince, and goes off to lush green Malaya, there is the feeling that Scott himself is daunted by the task of continuing to work this particular soil.

The later fifties were in fact difficult years for him. Then as now, his earlier literary achievements had not been fully recognized, and his responsibilities as a director of Higham's and as a family man both lay heavily on him. In one year alone (1958), he had to contend with a hospital stay for Penny, his father's death, and a traumatic falling out with the mother whom he had always struggled to please. Moreover, the amoebic disease which he had contracted in India, but which was not diagnosed until 1964, was worrying and debilitating, and he was drinking heavily. His marriage came under severe strain. Added to this was the suspicion that his main source of inspiration as a writer was growing unmarketable. *Sahibs and Memsahibs*, a play which finally was broadcast in 1958, had been hard to sell; he was beginning to believe something of Aubrey Menen's, which he quoted ruefully to the Commonwealth Countries' League later: 'India was a notorious bore' (*MAM* 91).

However, at the end of 1959, Scott's American publishers, William Morrow, stepped in with an offer of financial support for the next three years, and in 1960 Scott left his job to devote himself to writing. The move paid immediate dividends in his finest novel to date, *The Birds of Paradise*, in which the fall of the Raj reasserts itself as a potentially tragic theme. *The Bender* and *The Corrida at San Feliu*, which followed, show that his private demons were by no means quieted; the latter, in particular, confirms that by this stage it was hardly possible for Scott to express them in straightforwardly realistic terms. The problem of transcribing the everyday business of living was now an important part of his subject as a writer.

Shortly after this, Scott returned to India for the first time since the war. 'No idea why, except to recharge batteries' (*MAM* 166), he wrote later. The tactic worked: the seeds of *The Jewel in the Crown* (1966) were taking root in his mind before he even returned home. This first novel was followed by *The Day of the Scorpion* (1968) and *The Towers of Silence* (1972), and after two further trips to India the *Raj Quartet* was completed with the publication of *A Division of the Spoils*. His most ambitious work, the *Quartet* synchronizes a large number of intensely personal dramas not only with each other but also with the complicated political developments of the time. Its constant shifts of perspective make it resistant to thematic closure, a fact that should not raise doubts about Scott's stance on the key humanitarian issues, but which does establish his now typically postmodernist concern with the relativity and diversity of the historical 'truth'.

Sadly, the immense labour of writing the *Quartet* took a further toll on both Scott's marriage and his health, and by the time recognition finally came, with the award of the Booker Prize of 1977 for his tragi-comic addendum to the *Quartet*, *Staying On* (1976), he was too ill to enjoy it fully. His American launch parties and lecture trips had come to an abrupt end with a visit to a clinic in Tulsa, Oklahoma, on his 1977 return to the university where he had been a Visiting Professor only the year before. When the Booker award ceremony took place in London, he was still in Tulsa recuperating from an operation which was too late to save him from a losing battle with cancer. Although Penny was waiting for him on his return to England, there was little time to enjoy their reunion either. He died in the Middlesex Hospital, on 1 March 1978, at the age of 57.

The idea of India as a 'metaphor' for Scott has one last relevance: he missed not only the end of the real drama of the Raj, but also the final act of his own reconstruction of it. *Staying On* was televised on Anglia television in 1980, and *The Jewel in the Crown* was serialized by Granada in fourteen parts over the first three months of 1984. Both were widely acclaimed, with the latter being aired right across America and Europe, as well as in the former colonies (including both India and Bangladesh); it has since been repeated twice, most recently to mark the fiftieth anniversary of India's independence in 1997. To a writer whose own life was filled with conflict, and who was emphatic about not wanting to meet his readers in an area of *'bored neutrality'* (*MAM* 80), the controversy which it provoked in England would probably have come as less of a surprise than its remarkable world-wide success.[7] But the fact that dissent has been sharply polarized between supporters and detractors of empire suggests that, true to his original profession, Scott had in fact been able to present a balanced statement of accounts.

# 2

# Novels of the Fifties

Should a man's personal sympathies supersede his professional standards? At what point or on what surety should trust be allowed to banish reserve? On what values should a man base his life? From the very beginning of his career as a novelist, Paul Scott uses a complex play of unusual relationships, symbolic incidents and places, and varying points of view, to explore problems like these – the kind of problems he had faced in the army, and was facing again now as he established himself in the postwar world. Doing no more than hint at possible answers, he exercises a disturbing power over his readers from the start.

As *Lines of Communication*, the title of the original dramatic version of *Johnnie Sahib*, indicates, Scott's first published novel builds directly on his experience of helping to keep the 'lines' open for the allied troops driving the Japanese 'back into Burma and then out of Burma' (p. 9). The details of this operation, as an air supply company advances south from one air-strip to the next (the five parts of the novel take place on five different bases), and as changes are proposed in its organization by Lieutenant-Colonel Baxter from Calcutta, therefore have an almost documentary feel to them. But (as usual in Scott's work) this is misleading. What matters is the deeper sense in which the 'lines' have to be kept open. The task of mediating between Baxter and section captains like the eponymous Johnnie Brown falls to the company's major, and it is a tough one. Ironically, it is the dialogue which first indicates the *difficulties* of communication here:

> The Major stared uncomprehendingly at Prabhu, who smiled sadly and shook his head from side to side as if to say, 'All this is without meaning'.
>
> 'Who the hell is Colonel Baxter?'

'This I am not knowing, sir'.
'Then what is Colonel Baxter coming for?'
'This I am not knowing either, sir'.
'This you are not knowing either!'
'No, sir. We just had message to meet him at airfield'.
Prabhu wilted under the Major's steady gaze. (p. 11)

Prabhu, of course, knows exactly what Colonel Baxter has come for – to inspect the company – but he is reluctant to cause a last-minute flap. This is Scott in his lighter vein, one which would find its best expression in the verbal skirmishes of *Staying On*, and it is easy to see behind such passages as these the shadow of the radio script.

Against this background, however, a serious drama is enacted. It is not the kind of drama which readers might expect from a war novel: although it describes the company's movements, duties and discomforts, and brings out the loyalties and insecurities of young soldiers just behind the front line, there is no preoccupation with the issues of killing or being killed in battle. Instead, Scott sets out to probe the different approaches to leadership adopted by the three main characters: the Major, Johnnie, and Johnnie's new second-in-command, Jim Taylor.

The Major is a leader who has sacrificed his individuality to the requirements of his role, a sacrifice of which he himself is deeply aware. Johnnie, on the other hand, leads by virtue of his own personality. A larger-than-life figure, he is an unconventional leader who has handpicked the men in his section and believes that they follow him from personal loyalty. He eventually annoys the Major once too often, by refusing to make the section do an extra assignment at night, something which confirms the Major's suspicion that Johnnie's close relationship with his men has become counter-productive. After Johnnie has been sent back to the main base, his position is taken over by the more diffident and introspective Jim, who must strive to find his own approach to leadership somewhere between these two extremes.

However, Johnnie's ghost haunts his successor. In a final effort to exorcise it, Jim does something Johnnie would never have done: he insists on putting Johnnie's orderly, Jan Mohammed (the man whom Nimu had been teaching to read), on a supply flight from the airfield along with another man who suffers from air-sickness. The plane crashes and, in a symbolic crucifixion, the figure running away from it flings out his arms before being consumed by the fire.

Nothing could demonstrate more graphically the cost of abandoning Johnnie's individualistic approach to leadership; yet there is no return to old ways. Assured by Johnnie's old flame, the Eurasian nurse Nina (a rather pathetic figure), that Johnnie is happy in his new posting and is 'letting go' of his old unit (p. 207), Jim decides not to relinquish his command after the catastrophe, and is last seen walking briskly towards the Major's tent.

This decision, though, like the earlier one to put Jan Mohammed on the flight, seems to have less to do with the dialectics of leadership in the novel than with Jim's personal feelings about Johnnie. In fact, Johnnie has never stopped dominating the third-person narrative, even during his long absences from it, to the extent that both the Major and Jim have taken their substance largely from their responses to him. And though his humanity has been taken for granted throughout, there is something ambiguous about it: after all, the tenacity of his hold over his men has skewed not only the narrative, but Jim's own personality, provoking an act of unnecessary cruelty, and finally setting him on a course which may not be at all right for him.

Scott later came to associate *Johnnie Sahib* with 'an even earlier, more distant, *unpublished* period' (*MAM* 43); but it marks the first appearance in his novels of one of his favourite types: the man who exerts a disproportionate amount of influence on others, and particularly on *one* other vulnerable person. In subsequent novels, the two characters involved may be brothers, like Dwight and Joe MacKendrick in *The Alien Sky*, or they may be thrown together quite by chance, like Brian Saxby and Tom Brent in *The Chinese Love Pavilion*; class and racial tensions complicate matters, too, when Ronald Merrick confronts the public school educated Hari Kumar in the *Raj Quartet*.

This element in Scott's fiction, to which he returns obsessively again and again, may well have derived in part from some episode of victimization which took place during those traumatic early months in the army, before his marriage. But Scott clearly feared something hard and destructive in his own nature as well, something which threatened all that was sensitive and caring in him – an inner force which he associated with the *duende* or goblin-figure described by the Spanish poet and dramatist Lorca, and which he recognized in other writers besides himself. The *duende* is seen by Edward Thornhill in *The Corrida at San Feliu* as a 'little black hunchback' chained up inside the human heart, 'aching with the pain of his imprisonment and his deformity' (p. 117). In this first novel, both Jim Taylor and his author seem to hurry away baffled from their encounter with it; it would take time for Scott to recognize, analyse and contain the dangerous energy which here explodes so pointlessly over Jan Mohammed, and to involve the reader fully in his confrontation with it.

Scott would refine his treatment of the leadership theme in his fourth novel, *The Mark of the Warrior*; but immediately after *Johnnie Sahib* he turned his attention to the complicated social scene presented by the India he had experienced in Ranchi, a small hill station where he spent some of his last leaves in Bihar.

As might be expected from a book with a title derived from Maud Diver's famous *The Englishwoman in India* (1909),[1] *The Alien Sky* dispenses with officers, havildars and orderlies, and replaces them (for the first time in Scott's writing) with a gallery of colonial sahibs, memsahibs and their neighbours and acquaintances, who include Eurasian girls and a maharajah. The predominantly male ambience of Scott's first novel is seriously challenged, and love begins its gradual movement to the centre of his vision.

Here, the *duende* is mainly assigned to a figure who is physically absent throughout: Dwight MacKendrick was a young American who rose swiftly to the rank of colonel and died in the Pacific before the narrative begins. But again, this figure is the most powerful presence in the novel. The main character is his brother Joe, who is still under his fierce spell after having been physically and psychologically bullied by him as a child. Hardly knowing why, Joe has come to India just after the war to seek out Dwight's lover Dorothy, whose letters he had come across among Dwight's belongings. His search leads him to Marapore, where he finds the woman at last. She is married, as she was even when Dwight met her: her husband, whom she does not love, is Tom Gower, an idealistic man who runs an experimental farm nearby, but has just stirred up a hornets' nest by writing an editorial in the *Marapore Gazette* welcoming the concept of Pakistan. Against a backdrop of growing political tension, Joe discovers that the secret which made Dwight reject Dorothy in the end was not her inability to bear children, as he had supposed; rather, it was that she is one-fourth Indian.

Significant here is the way Scott's already established preoccupation with power begins to converge with his growing interest in both racial and emotional dilemmas (matters which were largely peripheral in *Johnnie Sahib*). On the social level, he shows a variety of reactions to the great changes now imminent in India – on the British side, the kind of 'anguish there was in being forced to hang on to what was already moving away, because there seemed to be no other support' (p. 47); on the Indian side, a resentment of further interference, well-intentioned or otherwise. As usual, however, the situation has its metaphorical dimension. At a deeper emotional level, Joe makes a conscious parallel between colonial circumstances and his own, when he looks around the room at Sanderson's 'fraternisation' party and asks himself, 'Which of these people here was a Dwight, and which a victim of someone like Dwight?' (p. 67). Of course, the one person he can actually identify as such a victim is Dorothy, whose happiness has been destroyed both by Dwight himself and the facts of her birth in colonial India. These two characters, with their confused identities and lost allegiances, recognize each other as fellow sufferers, but cannot heal each other: 'You're like me, aren't you? You haven't anywhere to go', Dorothy says to Joe, before his unsuccessful attempt to make love to her (p. 197).

There is no satisfactory resolution to the problems raised by this second novel, either. But in this case, the author himself clearly recognizes it, working through a complicated plot to an anticlimactic ending. Dorothy's secret has also been uncovered by Joe's disgruntled servant, Bholu. Bholu now embarks on an amateurish blackmail attempt, with disastrous results: taken for an activist as he approaches the Gowers' house ahead of a rioting mob of students, he is killed by Gower's assistant, John Steele; in an act of reckless retaliation, Steele himself is shot to death on his way to the inquest by the students' ringleader,

Vidyasagar. It is all rather melodramatic, and the stage now seems set for Joe to sweep Dorothy away, rescuing her from an increasingly problematic future. However, he is prevented from doing so – and thus from stepping into his brother's shoes – by her unhappy husband's suicide attempt. Dorothy goes back to Tom, and Joe sets off alone, still troubled by 'the distant cries of jackals' (p. 284), on the first leg of his return journey to the States. The contrast with the ending of *Johnnie Sahib*, where Jim Taylor strides with questionable confidence towards the Major's tent, is striking.

In fact, it does this novel no justice to strip it to its bones. As well as having a wider canvas and greater variety of characters than *Johnnie Sahib*, it substitutes for the simple geographical advance of the earlier novel a much more sophisticated intertwining of political and personal events. Dorothy is not an attractive character, and her dilemma is outdated, but the inhibitions and hostility which vitiate all her relationships are explored with subtlety and insight, not only through her own story but also through that of her Eurasian schoolfriend, Judith Anderson. It is a triumph of Scott's art that the reader sympathizes with her, as well as with her uncomprehending and increasingly wretched husband. Some of the surrounding figures, like the Maharajah's superannuated English governess, Miss Haig, or the hysterical Cynthia Mapleton, are stereotypical, and Sanderson's dreadful party recalls the bridge party – 'Indians, not cards', as Scott puts it later (*DSc* 451) – in Forster's *A Passage to India*. But the relationships at the heart of the novel are handled in a wholly original way and are deeply compelling.

If these relationships are not 'worked out' as some readers might expect, the clue might be found in a curious, rather overwrought passage towards the end of *The Alien Sky*. It expresses the feelings of the originally liberal and humane Tom Gower, when he goes to the jail to visit Vidyasagar. Under the pressure of his disappointment and distress, in both political and personal affairs, his humanity has been gradually eroded:

> And now that they were together Gower knew the real reason why he had come. He wanted to see the boy cower. He wanted the boy to fall on his knees and beg for mercy. And he wanted to beat his own hands on the bars, beat and beat until the skin was broken and the blood came and some of his own agony was released to enter into

> the boy. Hoarsely, he said, 'I came to see if there's anything I can do for you'. (pp. 254–5)

The *duende* cannot be shunted off to the side; nor is it only the leader, the bully or the writer who can give it expression. Gower's image of himself beating frantically on the prison bars shows that, given the appropriate circumstances, everyone has the potential for venting the hunchback's rage. This is something that Scott, like both Joe and Gower, was only just beginning to deal with.

In *The Alien Sky*, Dorothy Gower's plight largely mirrors Joe's; Scott is still mainly concerned with an unequal relationship between two men, which the weaker man is struggling to overturn. In these first two novels, there has also been a third man, somewhat outside that relationship, but on whom it impinges (the Major in *Johnnie Sahib*, Tom Gower in *The Alien Sky*). Scott's next work, *A Male Child*, is the first of his novels to be set in England. However, the basic pattern is very much the same, except that, in this case, the focus is placed firmly on the third party. Since this character is also the narrator, his difficulty in understanding the oddly triangular situation produces a powerful psychological teaser. But in a development of Nina's role in *Johnnie Sahib*, the wife of one of the other two men helps to produce not a disappointing but a promising outcome.

At first, the prognosis seems gloomy enough. As in the previous novel, a young man has died in the war before the narrative opens. His name was Edward Hurst. Ian Canning, the narrator, is taken to stay at the Hursts' family home in Surrey, a house called Aylward, by Edward's surviving elder brother, Alan. Alan had been Ian's comrade in the Far East, and had found him alone and depressed in London, still suffering from bouts of the obscure tropical fever which had led to his discharge from the army. At Aylward, Ian finds himself oddly mistaken for Edward by the elderly and demanding Mrs Hurst; he is then pressured into filling her dead son's vacant slot in the family. As might be imagined from a novel filled with shadows of the past, humour is in short supply here: at the beginning, Ian is thinking of suicide; in the last chapter, he tells his estranged wife that his disease has finally been diagnosed, and is one which is as yet incurable.

Nevertheless, and not entirely unexpectedly, the narrative closes on an upbeat note. Alan's wife Stella, who had left him shortly before he bumped into Ian in London, has returned pregnant with their child to Aylward. In a memorable scene, the older Mrs Hurst is shown looking downstairs in bafflement at the white-faced girl with her shining hair. Ian takes care of Stella during Alan's frequent absences, something which seems inevitable in view of the fact that Stella had originally loved Edward. The eventual birth of a son and heir to Alan and Stella therefore confirms to Ian as well as to Alan that 'There's everything in the world to live for' (p. 224). More importantly, it also releases Ian from his role as a replacement for Edward (the original son and heir). He prepares to leave Aylward with a certain guarded optimism: 'A chapter was ended. A new one would begin in the morning' (p. 221).

The questions this novel raises are legion. It is not clear, for instance, which of the brothers in Scott's central *alter ego* dyad had been the dominant one. Was Alan really cruel to Edward as a child, as his mother supposes? Their older half-cousin Adela says he was not; and Stella recalls Edward's confession that it was he who used to get Alan in trouble. Then, why does Alan bring Ian home? Is it the act of a good Samaritan – or is it to hurt his mother with the likeness to his dead brother? Mrs Hurst suspects so, and why else should a chilling and 'curious expression' cross Alan's face when Ian mentions her reaction to his appearance (p. 121)? But perhaps Alan just wants to satisfy himself that he could have got on with the grown-up Edward, had he survived the war. Or perhaps Alan has grown tired of being the only son, and wants Ian to take on what he considers to be Edward's responsibilities. Mrs Hurst and Adela, in particular, raise a host of contradictory possibilities about Alan for Ian (and, just as importantly, the reader) to ponder.

But Ian himself is even more intriguing than either Edward or Alan, and emerges as separate from both of them in the end. There is always some question as to whether he is as much like Edward in appearance as Mrs Hurst says: Adela notices only the 'vaguest facial resemblance' (p. 119). The idea of their similarity may perhaps have been foisted on Ian by the other family members' needs. He does take over from Edward in some ways, but this could be because the hand-me-down life he is offered at

Aylward is all he can cope with after the trauma of the war, and in his present state of health. Or he may genuinely wish to avoid the temptation of 'living easy' there by helping the family in whatever ways he can (p. 151). At any rate, the shadows of the past clear at last: he, who once 'put no value upon the sentiment of family ties' (p. 85), comes to admire Alan for willingly resuming his marriage bonds, and rejoices with him and Stella in the advent of a new life. And the future he is starting to face in the last chapter is all his own.

Seen from this point of view, the novel reflects something more than Scott's own early postwar depression. He may well have been feeling then that 'The lucky ones died. The rest of us stayed on to face the futility' (p. 189). But what exercised him much more (and much more productively now) was how a man was to establish himself in the new order: how he was to know whom to trust, how far he could trust himself, and what kind of relationships (male and/or female) he could commit himself to. Since Ian comes to believe in Alan, have faith in his own integrity, and feel some sympathy for both his wife and (especially) Stella, the title refers not only to the male heir who replaces him and helps to free him from the Hursts' influence, but to the projection of the more self-confident, more caring male into the unknown future.

Like its predecessors, this novel is not without its flaws. It is entirely appropriate that a narrative set largely in an old house now divided into flats, and dealing with the anxieties of a protagonist who needs to break out of it, should often seem stifling. But it is unnecessarily so. Restricted by his first-person narrative, Scott has overloaded the earlier dialogues with information, and the pace is also slowed by complications involving peripheral characters like the tenants of Ian's London flat. Moreover, Scott's presentation of pregnancy is ambivalent: for much of the time, 'this bloody womb business' seems designed as a kind of trap for men and women alike (p. 155), a troubling view for a work which depends so much on childbirth for its positive ending. But by constantly presenting alternative views about his main characters and their complex relationships, Scott skilfully and very deliberately involves his readers in the various dilemmas of manhood. It is the first time he has asked so much of them. That he manages to leave them with something very like hope declares him to have been one of the most promising figures in the postwar literary scene.

In Scott's next novel, *The Mark of the Warrior,* he returns to his army experiences, and replaces the haunted rooms of Aylward with the dim, mysterious forests of western India. But again, the main characters to be set against this brooding backdrop are three men – a dead soldier, his younger brother, and a third man who has become deeply involved with both. And again, there is a woman whose character is not as fully developed as the men's, but whose role is significant. This pattern is now used to explore with a new precision the theme of leadership which Scott had previously tried his hand at in *Johnnie Sahib.*

That the role of the male continues to be Scott's basic concern is suggested by the 'Argument' with which the novel is prefaced: 'Three things are to be considered: a man's estimate of himself, the face he presents to the world, the estimate of that man made by other men. Combined, they form an aspect of truth'. Yet it is also clear that Scott is now very interested in the kind of corrective to this 'truth' which perhaps only a woman can supply.

The jungle itself plays a major role in this narrative. It made a profound impression on so many of those who went to serve in the subcontinent during the war.[2] Major Colin Craig in Scott's novel is a professional soldier who has been in India for eighteen years, but the risk of sudden death in the forests thick with undergrowth still frightens him, as it frightens most of his men. There are some, though, for whom the jungle is different. It offers the opportunity to kill, which is more important to them than the risk of being killed. They have a feeling for the terrain, and can sense the presence of the enemy. Craig can recognize such men now, men who bear 'the mark of the warrior'.

It was exactly this 'mark' which had distinguished John Ramsay, Craig's subaltern in the Burma campaign. In a brief prologue to the novel, it is explained that while Craig himself was engaged in a difficult river crossing during their retreat to India, John had been one of those already on land who had come under enemy fire; he had died of a stomach wound later that night. Part 1 opens about seven months later, when Craig, who has recovered physically but not mentally from the retreat, is resuming duties as the commander of a new company training for jungle warfare. But the past returns to haunt him in the shape of John's younger brother Bob, in his first batch of cadets.

In a narrative which the author is no longer at any pains to hide his role in, Craig's and Bob Ramsay's points of view are given alternately in sections headed 'Craig (5)', 'Ramsay (6)' and so forth. The core of the action is the training exercise outlined at the beginning of Part 2 which Bob is encouraged to plan, and subsequently put in charge of. Clearly, Craig is trying to exorcise his guilt about John's death, and to compensate for his own weaknesses, by turning Bob into the kind of consummate leader his brother had been. The plan succeeds, insofar as the younger brother too proves to have 'the mark of the warrior'; but in the process, further weaknesses are discovered in Craig himself and also in the 'warrior' mentality. It appears, for instance, that during the Burma retreat Craig had been unable to put John Ramsay out of his agony by shooting him, as perhaps he should have done. In general, he lacks the cold professionalism that a good officer needs. On the other hand, from his conversations with Craig and his growing understanding of the exigencies of jungle warfare, Bob Ramsay comes to suspect that his brother had intended a raft carrying the non-swimmers to disintegrate during the river crossing in Burma, 'to get rid of the weaklings' p. 212). And in proportion as Bob himself gains competence under Craig's direction, it is clear that he is developing a similar ruthlessness.

Much is made of the living Ramsay's progress from a sense of responsibility towards his fellow cadets, towards this kind of inhumanity. At first, he senses the others on his training exercise merging into his own identity: 'he felt the great weight of them as if it were a weight he carried in his own flesh, the great weight of a body which was his own and not his own but the body he must carry' (p. 211). Such a feeling was normal enough in the circumstances;[3] but then, caught up in what is after all only an exercise, he starts to drive the cadets mercilessly, and even insists that a havildar acting the part of a spy should be subjected to punitive treatment. The climax comes when a situation analogous to that in which his brother died develops: during a treacherous river crossing, Bob is trapped underwater, and drowned. Even worse than the responsibility Craig feels for and drowned. Even worse than the responsibility Craig feels for this second death is the other knowledge, the knowledge of what he has been doing to the living man, and, by extension, to others like him.

In the final version of the novel,[4] this is where Esther becomes important. Craig confesses to her afterwards, 'I thought I was helping him to be what I thought he had it in him to be, but he had other things in him as well and I let him destroy them'. 'What things?' asks Esther, puzzled. 'Things he needed. Things we all need', responds Craig (pp. 233–4). Then Esther seems to understand, and in the last sentence of the novel, Craig asks her to forgive him for having failed to provide *her* with them.

As usual, and now quite deliberately, the narrative leaves important questions unanswered. By engaging so fiercely in the training operation, did Bob Ramsay finally and triumphantly find his own (male) identity – 'the world which was himself, the world he had looked for' (p. 219)? It has certainly been claimed that 'our prevailing idea of masculinity tells men that violence is the *only* way for them to make contact with and draw strength from a crucial part of their innermost selves'.[5] Or, by crossing 'the barrier which separated the one reality from the other' (p. 195), did the young cadet simply lose his sanity?'[6]

In the revised ending of the novel, however, Craig's soul-searchings take the reader right outside the mind-set of the committed soldier, and turn the rehearsal for jungle warfare into a rehearsal – or metaphor – for life itself. Craig's words to Esther are vague, but they align him with a newer, softer post-war version of masculinity, implying that it is a mistake for a man to reject, as evidence of weakness, the very qualities on which he should be building his life. Thus, what Scott said in the introductory 'Argument' is now confirmed: the face a man presents to others, what those others think of him, and even what he thinks of himself, combine only to make 'an aspect of truth'. Bob Ramsay led his fellow cadets, gained their grudging respect, and died with a sense of fulfilment; but Craig, who is to some extent implicated in the cadet's tragic death, realizes at last that there are other standards by which a man can be judged; and that if he does not live according to them, he may indeed need forgiveness.

The first of Scott's novels to be published by Morrow, *The Mark of the Warrior* was a landmark in his literary career. The splitting of the focus between Ramsay and Craig was a first exercise in the narrative manipulations which would greatly enrich his later work, and the probing and suspenseful reconstruction of one dramatic episode in the past was another metafictional technique upon which he would want to elaborate. The process of writing was beginning to feature as a part of the plot itself. But this work is not just a step towards Scott's later achievements. Having drawn his readers into the frightening landscape of war and human aggression, Scott now shows them a small beacon of humanity. Its light comes mainly from Esther Craig, normally a solid and comforting presence in the background, but the source of one of the novel's most vivid images. On his first anxious 'recce' of the training exercise terrain, her husband comes on her waiting in the shade, reading the map, her hair glowing (like Stella Hurst's); and at this moment he feels the first authentic 'sharp, small stab of love' of all Scott's heroes (p. 73).[7]

# 3

# Novels of the Early Sixties

By the end of the fifties, Scott had already written *The Chinese Love Pavilion*; it was published in the autumn of 1960. Among the works that followed in the next few years, *The Birds of Paradise*, in which the Indian connection is most strongly maintained, has been most highly rated. But *The Bender* and *The Corrida at San Feliu*, the former set in England and the latter inspired largely by Scott's holidays on the Costa Brava, are more striking both technically and for the escalation in them of Scott's struggle with the 'handicap at love'.

In *The Chinese Love Pavilion* itself, the female figure in Scott's growing constellation of important characters is already developed enough to make a real challenge to the dominant, though often absent male 'other'. Indeed, the susceptible hero of this novel, Tom Brent, is pulled this way and that between the two.

This is all the more remarkable in view of the fact that Johnnie Sahib and the dead brothers of Scott's last two works pale into insignificance beside the eccentric Brian Saxby. The novel is worth reading for this figure alone. A botanist travelling in the Far East, Saxby is anything but elusive at first: hefty, red-bearded and overbearing, he has a strong physical presence. It seems inevitable that Tom should seek guidance and inspiration from him, because, in proportion as Saxby is more flamboyant than characters playing similar roles in the earlier novels, Tom's identity is even shakier than that of any of Scott's past heroes. An orphan with a family background of colonial service, he has worked his way out to India for the very purpose of trying to establish this identity. Tom's humorous account of his struggles to penetrate the fabric of Indian society is suddenly interrupted by the arrival of Saxby at his cheap boarding-house, appropriately enough during a terrific thunderstorm.

Recognizing Tom's fascination with the land, as he generally recognizes others' dreams, Saxby encourages him not to give up on India, but to stay and work its soil. Tom follows his advice, and again there is a splendid account of Tom's struggle to farm an infertile valley alongside the old India hand, Greystone – work reminiscent of Tom Gower's at his experimental farm in *The Alien Sky*, and equally doomed to disappointment. In a novel littered with shattered dreams, Greystone's obsessive well-sinking does nothing but use up all their resources. Tom's subsequent pursuit of Saxby in Malaya, where the older man devotes himself first to plant-collecting and then to a vendetta against Japanese soldiers who have destroyed his orchids, occupies the best part of the remaining narrative. Despite having been badly wounded in action himself, Tom eventually joins a detachment of British soldiers in the area of Saxby's clandestine operations, in an effort to locate him and save him from reprisals. The saving of Saxby is another dream that is doomed to failure.

For, typically, just when some kind of resolution might be expected, Scott's narrative only becomes more complicated. Major Reid, who commands the detachment, is the inevitable third man in the early Scott's three-cornered struggle for a male role. Driven and simultaneously tortured by a need to make others re-enact his own dehumanizing experiences as a professional soldier, Reid is impotent himself, but encourages his men to patronize a brothel run in the pavilion of the title. As indicated in a brief prelude to the main narrative, a love affair develops between Tom and the exotic Eurasian prostitute who runs the brothel. And Teena Chang, with her mixed racial and cultural background, her Chinese moods and her European moods, turns out to be almost as charismatic as Saxby himself. Since Saxby has visited Teena in the pavilion too, demanding her help in his vendetta, Tom's two extraordinary relationships slide together at this point.

The pavilion is not at all a promising venue for such a convergence. Scott depicts it in detail, but it is as much a symbolic structure as the haunted Aylward in *A Male Child*, and as closely associated with death: the Chinese merchant who originally built it was executed by the invading Japanese, who had carried out further executions in front of it; and a Japanese officer had committed suicide there, probably out of love for Teena. The obscure knitting of death with desire is confirmed when Tom gives Teena as a love-gift a jewelled *kris* or dagger which he had bought in Singapore; and the guilt consequent on the desire is suggested when he later compares the chambered pavilion, with its anteroom featuring a mosaic of dancing dragons, to the human heart.

In the event, Tom fails to save not only Saxby but Teena also; he is even obscurely implicated in their deaths. Saxby dies after a struggle with his Chinese follower, who had tried to attack Tom, and the only thing which is not doubtful about Teena's murder/suicide is that the instrument of death is the gorgeous but dangerous *kris*.

As for Saxby, who had tipped from eccentricity into destructive self-delusion, his death might be considered favourable to Tom's development: the younger man is put in the position of a 'magician's stooge emerging from a box at the climax of an illusion' (p. 31). But unfortunately, 'the flower dreamer, the *shaman* of the red beard' is as compelling on his deathbed among his overgrown plants as he was in life (p. 299). After all, 'I would have had Saxby no different' (p. 326), Tom muses. It is clear from this that what stopped Tom committing himself to Teena, and protecting her from her fate, was that strange prior attachment which still haunts him.

David Lodge has pointed out the tendency of postmodernist novelists to present the reader 'with more data than he can synthesize',[1] and Scott himself has Tom say at the end of the novel, 'they are only fallacious arguments that would produce a pattern out of the sad jumble of our dreams' (p. 326). But when Scott referred to *The Chinese Love Pavilion* later as 'a bit of a hybrid' (*MAM* 116), he seems to have had in mind some basic division in it. Between India and Malaya, perhaps, or between reality and illusion (madness, it would seem, in Saxby's case)? Or between the claims on Tom by Saxby and Teena? This last is the most interesting possibility. The pull exerted on the hero by the woman is certainly significant, even if Tom knows that he has failed to respond to it adequately in the end; the need for a new kind of commitment is strongly felt here.

Up to now, and even in *The Chinese Love Pavilion* itself, Scott's young heroes have felt that kind of attachment mainly to another man. But from a psychoanalytical, specifically Lacanian point of view, the mysterious 'absent other' which features in these early novels does not simply represent the object of desire; it also represents, by its very 'otherness', the prohibition of desire.[2] Failure to reunite with it, therefore, implies something more than a masochistic battle of self-denial on the author's part; it suggests also an acceptance of separation, which is a healthy outcome of the struggle to define the independent self. The emergence of a stronger hero like Ian Canning in *A Male Child*, the willingness of the middle-aged Craig in *The Mark of the Warrior* to share his problems about the Ramsay brothers with his wife, and the sidelining of much of the psychic cost to a relatively minor character like Major Reid in *The Chinese Love Pavilion*, are all signs that such a positive process is indeed at work. During this process, whether by instinct or as a matter of choice, Scott comes to feel that an essential attribute of identity is the capacity to offer 'unselfish' as against dependent or possessive love to a woman (*JS* 206).

Dora Salford is the name of the girl who first stirs the heart of William Conway, the narrator/protagonist of Scott's next novel, *The Birds of Paradise*. It happens during his childhood in India, and in contrast to the episodes involving the beguiling Teena Chang, the romantic incidents described here are quite innocent and uncomplicated. The nostalgia surrounding them extends initially to the whole evocation of the Indian experience, which takes place mainly before independence, when the Raj as well as the maharajahs still gloried in 'their finery and high-flown postures' (p. 243).

William first meets Dora, the daughter of a Major in an Indian infantry regiment, when he is 10. It is at a garden party thrown by the Maharajah of Tradura, one of the six princely states to which his father serves as the crown's Political Agent. The most significant experience of William's boyhood, before he is shipped off to school in England and shunted into the business world, is the moment of communion he feels with Dora on an annual big-game hunt. The two venture into a jungle clearing alone, and William has the main objective of the expedition, the majestic Kinwar tiger, within his sights. But in the face of her awe, 'lust for the animal's blood drained away' (p. 71). After the incident, he drops out of the hunt to keep Dora company at the lodge, 'divided in himself, not sure that sitting with a girl while there was man's business afoot was really what I wanted' (p. 72). Later, he gets a terrific flogging at his father's behest, apparently for acting like a coward. However, his behaviour on subsequent occasions quite absolves him from this, and there is no question but that what happened then was good and right: Dora had saved him from being 'soiled' by his blood-lust (p. 71). The humanizing influence of the feminine is felt very keenly here.

What is more, this first emotional involvement is something which remains when almost every other value in William's exotic past has been shown to be illusory. Not long after going through a divorce in England, he takes a sabbatical in the Far East, to rediscover this past (and, indeed, himself): 'When there's no duty as such to go back to, going back becomes a duty in itself' (p. 259). Chance reunites him not only with Dora, but also with the third of their little childhood group – Krishanramarao, or Krishi, who has now succeeded his father as the Maharajah of Jundapur, another of the territories which had once been in the purview of William's father. As the three disillusioned middle-aged people stand again within a huge cage of stuffed exotic birds in which they once played as children, William's tenderness for Dora is reawakened. And it is not just for the Dora of the past; she is endeared to him too by 'all the traces left upon her by her years, for her years were her life, and I had loved her as a child' (p. 246).

The dead birds themselves, from which the novel takes its title, provide a wonderfully phantasmagoric setting for this new/old illumination. Considered footless in legend, and rendered footless in fact by trappers, these inhabitants of 'the airy realms of paradise' are at once richly symbolic (of the Raj which was dying even then in William's childhood, despite all appearances; of the princely states like Krishi's Jundapur, which were to meet a similar fate; of elusive dreams cruelly netted by the realities of life), and an actual background against which past and present are suddenly united (p. 247). The birds must be rotting even on the outside now, without the elaborate care their plumage used to receive, just as the real birds of paradise are dying out in the wild because of cruel exploitation. There is already an 'ancient dampness', a 'warm and cloying' smell inside the overgrown cage (p. 244). Eventually, nothing of this potentially grotesque scenario will remain, except the memory of the exotic past – and the love which briefly blossomed within it, and can still inspire the human heart.

In the many-layered, highly self-conscious narrative of *The Birds of Paradise,* such love is set in contradistinction to three other backgrounds all tangentially connected to the central motif: the chilly, loveless world which William has recently left behind in London, once the hub of empire; the POW camp in which he himself was 'caged' for over three dreadful years during the war, and where he almost had to have his own feet amputated; and a pacific island called Manoba, from which the birds of paradise have now disappeared. Manoba is the place to which William has come in order to meet Dr Daintree, a dedicated medical researcher about whom he had learned from the doctor at his POW camp. At first sight, this mission is as unproductive as Tom Brent's final search for Saxby in Malaya; but it yields more insights. Indeed, William's whole story is told in the form of his reflections from the island, from which he has yet to return at the end.

It is apparent from these reflections that the 'absent others' of this story are William's cold father from his Indian childhood, as well as the now curmudgeonly and alcoholic Daintree himself. Although the narrative is too densely peopled and intricately crafted for either of them to dominate it completely, they have not lost their hold over the hero: William recognizes that in both there has burned 'the likeness of a noble aspiration' (p. 262), and he responds to this, wishing he had understood his father better during his lifetime, as he now understands Daintree. However, there is more acceptance and more hope here. The lost ideals, the now voiceless and moribund birds of paradise, are effectively relegated to the past by Dora and Krishi's gift to him, an obstreperous, vivacious parrot. This is not just the comic substitution that it seems: calling his name over and over, and singing a tender love-song, the parrot dispels the darkness that falls 'when the illusion is gone' (p. 262), reminding William of his own identity, and his own potential for love. The hope is that he will return from his sabbatical more mature, more self-aware, and demanding from life not a livelihood among 'suckers and munchers' like his materialistic ex-wife (p. 261), but a relationship with someone who can touch him as Dora has done.

This novel (which contains a host of engaging minor characters, such as the young William's governess, 'Canters', and tutor, 'Gray Hum') is often seen as a foretaste of the still more complex *Raj Quartet*. Certainly, it shows a gathering of Scott's powers, both technical and emotional. But as a narrative about one man's journey of self-exploration and -discovery, it is different in kind from the later work. It is deeply moving in its own right, placing first love at the very centre of the hero's experience, and establishing it as a powerful source of inspiration even amid the multiple demands and disappointments of later life.

There are signs in Scott's next two novels of India's continuing hold on his imagination: for example, George Spruce's youngest brother Guy in *The Bender* is living with (and being unfaithful to) Anina MacBride from 'Islington-pore'; and Edward Thornhill, the American novelist-hero suffering from writer's block in *The Corrida at San Feliu*, turns to India several times for alternative backgrounds to his characters' stories. But the other very specific locales which these narratives feature, and their different moods – ranging from wry to totally despairing – do seem to mark out both works as departures from the 'sequence' leading up to the *Raj Quartet*. They are apt to be set aside as, respectively, 'English'[3] and partly 'fake Hemingway',[4] when in fact they deal more consciously and urgently than ever with Scott's major concerns: the hero's search for his identity and the development of his capacity to love.

Chapter 1 of *The Bender* opens with a telephone conversation between Lady Butterfield and the eldest son of her late husband's cousin: 'I've been in the country for a bit', says George, explaining his absence from her Thursday soirées. 'The country? I hope you aren't in any kind of trouble', replies Lady Butterfield waspishly (p. 7). The Wildean rhythms are entirely appropriate, for George Spruce is the black sheep of the family in what is, superficially, a comedy of contemporary manners. He has been drifting along pretty harmlessly up to now, on the modest interest of Sir Roderick Butterfield's legacy (the principal of which is intended for his own heir), but he did once need bailing out by his younger brother Tim after an episode of embezzlement; and he does need help again now, because this brother, an accountant, is pressing him urgently to repay the debt. This, it appears, is to deal with an unexpected family problem: Tim's unwed teenage daughter Gillian has become pregnant by a feckless plumber's mate. George of course has no immediate means of repaying Tim, and realizing that nothing is to be got from Lady Butterfield, he goes into a flat (alcoholic) spin. There is a good deal of bleak humour here: at one point, he tries to ring God (GOD 1961) from a telephone in a night-club called The Apocalypse on the Charing Cross Road.

But the potential for tragedy is very close to the surface. George may be a scapegrace, but he is neither selfishly on the make like Tim, nor aggressively up-and-coming like Guy. Anina, with her canny ways and 'most peculiar manner' of speaking (p. 8), quickly and correctly christens him 'Sweet-George'. He cares deeply for Gillian, who is his godchild as well as his niece. During his 'bender', he engages in some solemn heart-searching and decides that his best option is to commit suicide. This way, Gillian, as his younger brother's eldest child, will inherit Sir Roderick's money when she really needs it. But on the very same night that George contemplates driving into a tree in a stolen car, Gillian too thinks of a drastic solution to her problem. She attempts a do-it-yourself abortion, not because she does not want her baby, but because, on the contrary, an earlier interview with George has made her realize that she would never be able to go through with an adoption.

Fortunately, however, both disasters are averted. Two observant and not unkindly police patrolmen set George safely on his way to Tim's; and by the time he arrives there, Gillian is tucked up in bed, recovering. As in *A Male Child*, the prospect of an heir produces a happy ending: an arrangement is reached whereby George will fulfil his godfatherly duties, and see Gillian through 'the whole business' in a quiet cottage in Wales (p. 218). Appearances notwithstanding, George is no fool, and suspects that he is probably being used to help sweep the matter under the carpet. Still, he is genuinely delighted to accept a responsibility which will give meaning to his life as perhaps nothing else could. There is more satisfaction than ambivalence about his thoughts at the end: 'I didn't remember to ask what happens when she sees the baby. Which is the point, I mean, isn't it? Basically the point?'(p. 220). Since he himself is infertile after an attack of mumps, it is highly likely that Gillian's child will one day stand to inherit Sir Roderick's legacy.

Matters of work, money and social status are all deeply problematic in this novel of urban, middle-class life; but underlying them is the usual situation in which a weak hero has suffered from feelings of inadequacy since childhood. Quite simply, Mrs Spruce had fussed over Tim and loved him more than George. Yet there would be no point at all in George's trying to step into either of his more successful brothers' shoes. Their triumphs are seen to be as superficial as George's failures. Two important truths now emerge: that 'there's a limit to the amount of blame you can put on other people for what kind of man you are' (p. 192); and that what must be filled is not someone else's place after all, but the void within. Here, the first step towards filling it must be to opt out of a society in which, as Guy says bitterly after his unsatisfactory bedding of a starlet dubbed Antigone, 'Nobody is ever loved and everybody is always used' (p. 175); the next is the one which Scott is now proposing with more and more conviction – to care for someone else without any ulterior motives. This is exactly how George cares for Gillian, for whom he had been ready to give up life itself.

Again, this is only the skeleton of a narrative which is amply, perhaps too amply, fleshed out with the three brothers' whole family history, the full story of Tim's disloyalty to his accountancy partner, and a wide range of peripheral characters, among them the insouciant plumber's mate. Moreover, in what is now Scott's characteristic fashion, it is not told sequentially, but pieced together from dialogues, memories (including George's dying Aunt Ada's) and inner communings. There is even an overheard tape-recording, as George is given an opportunity to listen to Lady Butterfield's latest ramblings on her Grundig. As far as the action is concerned, Chapter 36 is a fair sample of Scott's mature technique. Here, concurrently, George sees Anina back to her Camden Town bedsit; Tim dines expensively with his wife on the strength of his lucrative but morally questionable job offer; Guy has his meaningless fling with 'Antigone'; Gillian sips gin and sinks down woozily into her boiling hot bath; and just about everyone else in the novel puts in a brief appearance. These juxtapositions capture both the fragmentation and contiguity of life in 'this drowned city' (p. 184); but, as the brilliant vignettes pile up, there is a sense in which not only the characters but the readers too are struggling for the air of wider spaces.

The growing crowdedness of Scott's vision seems to have gone with the gradual opening up of the patterns of his characters' relationships. It could hardly be accommodated in a single novel; but he had one more very deliberate try, in *The Corrida at San Feliu*. Ironically, in a work whose novelist-hero has been suffering from the dreaded writer's block, the possibilities come rushing in again from all directions, and it is the triumph of the real author that they are made to cohere and even illuminate. It is a courageous book, one in which the redemption of love seems almost too much of a miracle to hope for; a miracle, nevertheless, in which the reader senses that it is vital to continue believing.

Edward Thornhill is the unhappy novelist. He and his wife Myra have been staying in Spain, and, as the preface explains, the pieces which make up the novel were found in his study after their fatal car accident. Suspicions of a suicidal/murderous motive in the accident are aroused by the longest, autobiographical fragment, 'The Plaza de Toros': this reveals that Thornhill was distraught not only over his work, but also over Myra's affair with a handsome young Spaniard. The long description of a bullfight in this part actually owes little to Hemingway: like George's 'bender', it is largely an occasion for soul-searching. The spectacle of this kind of manliness in action, 'of the stature man can achieve when he spices his civilised intelligence with primitive blood-lust' (p. 288), does not thrill Thornhill as it had thrilled Hemingway; there is more repulsion than admiration in his account of it, and more self-disgust than either. He identifies in turn with the ruthlessness of the matador, the callousness of the crowd, and the agony of the victim baffled by the misleading swirls of the cape. As for the fictional fragments about human relationships, these show similar responses as Thornhill tries desperately to deal with his own situation through stories of betrayal, cruelty and shame.

The first, 'The Leopard Mountain', establishes betrayal as the main problem. A powerful piece set in Africa, it deals with a junkyard foreman who ends up shooting the employer who has ruined him. The subsequent fragments principally involve a couple called Thelma and Bruce Craddock, and Thelma's love affair with a much younger man, Ned Pearson. Thelma is alternately beautiful and plain, and the setting shifts from India to Spain and back again. In the end, both his wife and the novel are evidently too much for Thornhill. The only relief in these fragments comes from a brief, wistful scenario in which he and Myra are projected 'into a [romantic] future that was never theirs' (p. 246), and a contrasting, desperate, apocalyptic finale immortalizing Thelma's passionate affair with Ned.

By its very nature, this novel is still more packed than *The Bender* with images and characters. Besides the faithless Thelma/ Myra, for instance, there are several women who have suffered innocently: Lesley, the unhappy daughter of the Clipsby-Smiths in 'The First Betrayal' and the neglected wife of Ned in 'The Arrival in Mahwar' (the two Indian fragments); Leela, the Eurasian princess in 'The Plaza de Toros' who was Craddock's first wife, and who drank powdered glass to escape from a life of ignominy and frustration; and Mitzi, the half-Jewish girl who was Thornhill's own first wife, and whose troubled background is most clearly explained in the preface. Mitzi had also committed suicide. All these briefly but vividly realized figures overlap with each other, and even, at some points, with Thelma and Myra. Another complication in the narrative is that, after Mitzi's death, Thornhill had taken Thelma from his cousin John, to whom she was originally engaged; his guilt was intensified when John died soon afterwards in an another suspicious-looking car accident. Along with this absent 'other' (a figure which continues to hover over Scott's work), Thornhill is more tenaciously haunted by the figure of the *duende,* who even appears as the hunchbacked ticket-tout for the *corrida.* This, along with the *corrida* itself, and the whole series of troubled and often suicidal characters which fills this work, is only another embodiment of his own spiritual malaise.

At first sight, *The Corrida at San Feliu* appears to be a work of self-flagellation, perhaps one into which Scott has poured his own accumulated guilt for 'betraying' his own wife by his choice of a writing career – and by the alcoholism, moroseness and self-doubts which went with it. Yet the narrative, which so painfully analyses the intolerable struggle with the artistic process, is not after all 'a private game' (p. 28). It demonstrates objectively how the creative imagination simultaneously grapples with the dark recesses of the heart, and is filled with endless alternatives for every word, action and feeling that occurs to it. The various casts of characters which present this struggle so graphically manage to catch and transfer the reader's sympathies until the longing for acceptance and love becomes almost unbearable. At the end, Bruce Craddock taunts his wife about Ned: 'He couldn't have cared much for you, really, could he?' She runs to her room, and cries, 'It isn't true. He did care. He did... He did! He did! And so did I' (p. 315). What she wants to believe is what everyone wants and needs to believe: that there is a reality 'behind the illusion that a man can care for someone other than himself' (p. 305). This is a reality which Thornhill cannot glimpse in the *corrida*, or in his own life. But Scott has shown again that it must be discovered, for neither men nor women can endure to live without it.

*The Corrida at San Feliu* is a challenging work, in which the process of structuring a text is an important part of the novelist's subject, and one in which the reader is expected to cooperate. In fact, the degree of cooperation required is unusual, even considered in the context of other postmodernist productions of the sixties like John Fowles' *The French Lieutenant's Woman* (1969), with its choice of endings. Yet, whilst incomplete correspondences and unresolved questions constantly lead readers to suspect that there are other interpretations besides their own, the rewards are there as well: as Thornhill tells Myra near the end: 'there is a sense, isn't there, of opportunity?' (p. 308). This pertains, too, to Scott's presentation of human nature here as contorted by guilt and frustration. Thornhill adds that he had once written about someone who was troubled by strange dreams: 'One day, the dreams went and he said, "Thank God, now I can have a bit of peace!" But he was wrong. He should have said: "Now I can begin to make discoveries"' (p. 309). The man's words about having 'a bit of peace' are taken from Thornhill's first novel, which is described in the preface; but the hopeful comment on them is a new and significant addition.

# 4

# The *Raj Quartet*: A Study in Narrative

Since Scott lists among Thornhill's earlier works 'a trio of novels about colonial life' (p. 26), he may already have had in mind the explorations which would yield his own discoveries. In June 1964, soon after coming back from his first visit to India since the war, he began writing what was to be the first volume of his own quartet on the same subject.

True to form, his starting-points were not ideas but images, almost cinematic in their vividness: as he explained later, one was that of a girl (who would become Daphne Manners) running; the other was that of a mission school superintendent (who would become Miss Crane) removing Gandhi's portrait from her wall. Scott then came up with another picture to which Miss Crane was attached: 'an old engraving showing Queen Victoria receiving tribute from representatives of her Indian empire' (*MAM* 64). The subcontinent itself was Victoria's greatest asset, and this gave him his first title, *The Jewel in the Crown*; and, although not in any simplistic way – for Miss Crane's impatience with Gandhi did not mean that she respected British policies – it admirably suggested his more negative themes of loss and change. But at the same time, the first image gave Scott something far more positive, something he had been seeking to formulate in his earlier novels. For the girl running, inspired by a rather lumpish young woman whom he had encountered in Calcutta in 1964, and who had been in love with an anglicized Indian, was 'strangely of good heart'; she had something about her which '*had not been changed by a bitter experience*'. With her 'great capacity for love', she represented 'something admirable in the human spirit' (*MAM* 60, 63–4).

Yet if Scott was already close to his 'discoveries', he still needed to work them out fully, and not just through the girl; and with one image yielding to countless others, and the burden of all that he knew and felt about India to be carried by both images and characters, there was more need than ever for structural organization of a very high order.

'NO IDEA THAT THERE WOULD BE *FOUR NOVELS*', claimed Scott after the publication of *A Division of the Spoils* (*MAM* 167); whether or not this was entirely true, a coherent narrative does evolve, moving slowly and with much (but never exact) recapitulation from the afternoon and evening of 9 August 1942 to nearly midnight on 9 August 1947; in other words, from the day after Gandhi's Quit India resolution to just before India's Independence Day (15 August 1947). What is remarkable about the *Raj Quartet* as a narrative process is its blend of simultaneity and progress; of history at once in the making and on the move; of major political events impinging through imaginary local ones on fictional people's lives – and of these characters themselves developing in response to them.

This blend is achieved in three main ways. The first is dependent on his strong feeling for the past and its enduring impact: he keeps prior episodes in play in the novel's present (as with the Burma retreat disaster in *The Mark of the Warrior*). The second enriches the texture of the narrative still more: it is his ability to deal with several casts of characters at once or to transfer the reader's sympathy to successive sets of characters (as he does in *The Corrida at San Feliu*). Then, in the service of these skills, there is his adroitness in bringing out the interconnections, by the kind of strategies employed to such good effect (but in too narrow a confine) in *The Bender* – strategies which on the one hand help to establish authenticity, but on the other, draw attention to the author as (along with the reader) a player in 'the game . . . called fiction' (*CSF* 29).

The historical past of Scott's narrative, which resonates so effectively all through it, is already implied in the images which first inspired him. But it is vital to distinguish between the original situations and the way Scott recreates and uses them for his own fictional purposes.

To start with Scott's first inspiration. The image of the girl running evokes all the horror of the great Mutiny of 1857–9. For Daphne Manners is running back to Lili Chatterjee's house in the fictional town of Mayapore, after having been subjected to a brutal gang-rape in the fictional Bibighar Gardens. The building that was once on this site had been destroyed by a Scotsman, who was later murdered by sepoys together with his wife and infant. Scott also directs the reader to remember 'that other Bibighar in Cawnpore' (*JC* 151), a real place which became the scene of the most notorious incident of the Mutiny, when over 200 British women and children were slaughtered there.[1] Coming the day after the Quit India motion, Daphne's ordeal can therefore be taken to symbolize savage retaliation for colonial oppression. It inevitably substantiates new fears of such a retaliation in Mayapore, and provokes a swift and heavy-handed response from police and army authorities.

However, Scott does not present so crudely the episode which is never 'lost sight of' in the four novels (*JC* 67). 'Bibighar' means 'the house of women', and, like the love pavilion of Scott's earlier novel, the fictional Bibighar has romantic associations – it was originally built by a prince for his courtesans.[2] Daphne is not at all the stereotypical pure and sheltered English maiden of the (English) historical imagination: she has had two lovers already in England, and just before the rape had given herself willingly to Hari Kumar, a young Indian brought up and educated in England as Harry Coomer, but recently forced to return to India by the bankruptcy and suicide of his father. The couple's sexual encounter was deeply meaningful, and they are still lying in a tender embrace when the group of rough villagers comes upon them. Since the rape is carried out not just to abuse Daphne, but both of them – Hari is forced either to witness or to close his eyes to it – the men's colour is not an important factor. Indeed, Daphne is 'reported as saying that for all she knew they could have been British soldiers with their faces blacked' (*JC* 172). The deed may well have been inspired by contempt for the kind of inter-racial sex which, as Indian versions of the Gardens' history suggest, has been occurring clandestinely ever since the British first came to India; but in fact the rapists' motives are never known, for the true culprits are never caught. What is sure is only that the rape in the Bibighar Gardens is an assault on love itself.

Another assault follows, this time from the British side. It is equally disgraceful and repugnant. After her rape, Daphne had crawled over to Hari, removed the rags with which he had been gagged and bound, and comforted him in his distress; it was Hari who then carried her to safety. But Ronald Merrick, the handsome young DSP (Deputy Superintendent of Police), who has proposed to Daphne himself, makes Hari a scapegoat for the rape – and this, despite Daphne's own refusal to say anything which might possibly incriminate him. Incarcerating him on the pretext of political activism, Merrick physically abuses and humiliates him. British attitudes to an uncooperative Daphne and her pregnancy are equally virulent. They are most disgustingly expressed by the woman who says that, in her place, she would have had an abortion 'and thrown the filthy muck to the pi-dogs' (*JC* 167).

This assault on love, with its complex historical, racial, and sexual elements, remains part of the fabric of the present throughout the long (over half a million words) narrative; its reverberations are both positive and negative.

On the positive side, right from the start Daphne herself defies 'the spoilers' (*JC* 497): true to Scott's original image of her, she remains 'strangely of good heart'. She carries her unborn child 'like a woman in a state of grace' (*JC* 171), and dies after giving birth to a half-Indian daughter. As in *A Male Child,* the birth itself is a powerful symbol of hope: to her aunt, Lady Manners, it is 'a miracle' (*JC* 508), and Daphne herself briefly greets her infant with a smile before she slips into unconsciousness. Lady Manners is later recognized by the retired missionary Barbie Batchelor as being 'proud' of her niece (*TS* 363); she brings up the baby, named Parvati, in seclusion on a houseboat in Kashmir, then in Rawalpindi. In Kashmir, she is visited by a thoughtful Sarah Layton, who in some ways takes over Daphne's own role in the *Quartet;* and in Rawalpindi by the sympathetic governor's aide, Captain Nigel Rowan, who finds the little girl 'enchanting' (*DSp* 595). Parvati's story is carried to its furthest point when she is seen seventeen years later at the home of Lili Chatterjee, where her mother had once stayed: she is shy but natural, studious and musically gifted, waving goodbye as she runs to her *guru* for lessons in the kind of music her mother had 'instinctively loved' (*JC* 450). Looking more Indian than English, she is nevertheless destined, perhaps, to 'sing in . . . western capitals' one day (*JC* 517).

Parvati is only glimpsed briefly, but, like Rushdie's Eurasian protagonist in *Midnight's Children* (1981), she represents the launch of the postcolonial world, a world which will no longer be as 'small. Hateful. Ingrown' as that of British India (*JC* 459). Named after the consort to the great god Siva, and already accompanied by a young male *tabla* player, she is given every prospect of fulfilment and love in it.

However, references to the Bibighar Gardens in the subsequent novels of the *Quartet* continue largely in connection with Ronald Merrick. If Daphne is the heir to women like Dora and Gillian who inspire love in the earlier novels, then Merrick is the heir to overpowering brothers like Dwight MacKendrick or eccentrics like Brian Saxby, figures who seem to haunt the narrative even during their absences from it. The original events of *The Jewel in the Crown* are constantly relived. In particular, in *The Day of the Scorpion* Hari reveals to Rowan in intimate detail how Merrick treated him in jail: the extent of his sado-masochistic and homosexual tendencies now becomes clear for the first time. Rowan then relays this interview to Sergeant Guy Perron at some length in *A Division of the Spoils*. Yet Merrick is in fact more present than absent. Besides this continual scrutiny of his past behaviour, his later fortunes are closely followed. Transferred to the Indian Army, he is maimed and disfigured in the act of dragging Teddy Bingham and his driver from a burning jeep. Teddy dies; later, Merrick is rehabilitated enough to marry Teddy's widow, Susan Layton – Sarah's psychologically unstable younger sister.

But there is no happy ending for Merrick. Like Saxby, this character who appears in various roles and different places meets a bizarre end. By now, he has taken to dressing himself up in private as a Pathan, a disguise he once found useful for his intelligence activities. Pathans, tribesmen from the north-west of India, are generally tall and sometimes blue-eyed, so the choice of garb is appropriate; that they are reputed to be predatory and inclined to homosexuality also makes it appropriate.[3] Preying on Merrick's homosexual proclivities, an unknown enemy sends young men to his compound. One night when Susan is away, he is found dead in their bedroom, clothed in his Pathan outfit; the word 'Bibighar' has been scrawled on the dressing-table mirror with the make-up stick used to darken his face. Since it is a culmination of several minor incidents related to the Manners episode, the ugly retribution is not entirely unexpected; it even seems to be one for which the increasingly driven and obsessive Merrick was himself waiting.

Merrick's fate is the more appropriate in view of the wretched lot of his original victim. Towards the end of the *Quartet*, an article under Hari's appropriate pen-name of Philoctetes (the brave archer abandoned by the Greeks because of his noxious wound) appears in the *Ranpur Gazette*. From this, and from Sergeant Guy Perron's attempt to look him up before leaving Mayapore, it is clear that Hari, once a popular pupil at the same English public school that Perron himself had attended, has been released from jail only into a state of anonymity, penury and disappointment. It seems that with this one sad 'loose-end' (*JC* 512), the event which is never 'lost sight of' in the narrative has finally worked its way out. And taken all in all it appears at last as an indictment not of Indian brutality (like the historical massacre at Cawnpore), but of the British Raj itself.

According to Scott, Daphne was inspired not only by the girl he saw in Calcutta, but also by the historical figure of Marcella Sherwood, a mission school superintendent, who was assaulted in 1919: 'LIKE MISS SHERWOOD SHE HAS BEEN ATTACKED' (*MAM* 166). However, it was Scott's second image, that of the disillusioned missionary, which really brought back the Sherwood affair. Again, it is useful to understand the significance of the original event. The attack on Miss Sherwood was the incident leading to General Reginald Dyer's order to fire without warning on thousands of unarmed Indian civilians gathered in an enclosed space (Jallianwallah Bagh) in Amritsar. The injured and dying were left untended in an episode which was generally acknowledged to be 'the blackest stain on [the Government's] record',[4] and which helped to provoke Gandhi's first non-cooperation motion of 1920. Just as the Quit India resolution evoked memories of the worst episode of the great Mutiny, so the crack-down on it evoked memories of this later but equally notorious and numerically far more damaging British atrocity. As before, Scott rakes up the ugly past and carries references to it right through the *Quartet*.

Again, more important here than the original outrage is Scott's handling of it. In his updated fictional version of the 1919 episode, it is once more (as in the case of Daphne and Hari) a double assault. Indeed, on 9 August 1942, it is the Bengali Mr Chaudhuri, a teacher chaperoning Miss Crane on her return from a routine visit to his school in Dibrapur, who is dragged out of the missionary's old Ford and beaten to death by rioters. But Miss Crane, having got out to remonstrate with the men, is also hit and pushed over an embankment. Like Miss Sherwood, she is reported to have 'narrowly escaped with her life' (*TS* 63, 95). Scott embellishes the incident not only by showing an Indian colleague suffering the brunt of the assault, but also by having Miss Crane struggle back to his mutilated body and hold his hand. In what can be seen as a final effort to dissociate herself from the causes which led to his death, the elderly missionary later immolates herself. Her dreadful experience, and some visits from the formidable Lili Chatterjee, have made her realize that 'to work to, and put her trust in, the formula of a few simple charitable ideas was not enough' (*JC* 78). In blurring the line between victim and victimized, Scott again establishes the extent of his sympathies.

The fatal assault on the road back to Mayapore, like the assault on Miss Sherwood, has awful repercussions for many others besides the one Englishwoman involved. It is what first puts the Mayapore authorities on red alert. After this and the rape in the Bibighar Gardens, troops welded into 'a well-trained fighting machine' by Brigadier-General Alec Reid are keyed up to use violence against a much larger mob of rioters protesting the internment of Hari and five other so-called 'suspects' (*JC* 303, 331). This takes place in the narrow space of the Mandir Gate Bridge road, and clearly echoes the Jallianwallah Bagh massacre itself. But again, the issue becomes more complex here. Merrick, whom Reid had 'instinctively liked' (*JC* 311), is also implicated, because part of the crowd is made up of rioters retreating from his own armed charge on a mob at the railway station. Thus, some of those who drown when they throw themselves off the bridge to escape Reid's onslaught have already been wounded by Merrick's men. The spectacle of 'civilised intelligence' spiced with 'primitive blood lust' is never a pleasant one (*CSF* 288).

It is Reid – who reminds readers of the savage Major Reid in

*The Chinese Love Pavilion*, and whose surname is also noted to be a backwards form of Dyer's (*TS* 82) – who is held responsible here. He is soon shunted off, not into retirement on half-pay as Dyer was, but into preparations for active service in Burma. The transfer puzzles Nicky Paynton, wife of an army officer already in Burma, when she reads about it in the *Ranpur Gazette* two novels down the line, in *The Towers of Silence*.

For, while memories of the heyday of the Raj become fainter, those of the atrocities involved in it become more and more disturbing. The allegorical picture of the tribute to Queen Victoria reappears, it is true, to be handed down from one character to another; but only in Barbie's smaller copy of Edwina Crane's presentation piece. But the very name 'Jallianwallah' reverberates ominously throughout the *Quartet*. Hari, that other victim of the Raj, is arrested after Daphne's rape, at his aunt's house in the similar-sounding Chillianwallah Bagh. Later, in the hill station of Pankot, the elderly twice-widowed Mabel Layton, who once defiantly contributed to a fund for Dyer's victims, murmurs what sounds like 'Gilliam [remembered as Gillian] Waller' in her sleep (*TS* 95). Mabel's father, two husbands and stepson have all devoted their lives to the empire, but Mabel herself is assailed by the dreadful suspicion (even, now, conviction) that such efforts have all been misguided – worse, downright cruel. The Jallianwallah Bagh massacre itself is last mentioned in the penultimate chapter of the *Quartet*, in connection with Merrick's death (*DSp* 620).

Thus, as much as the rape with its echoes of the century-old Mutiny, the Mandir Gate Bridge road affair, with its echoes of the more recent massacre, is a part of the burden of the past which is never forgotten in the novels. Just as the two were linked in Scott's mind when he started to write, so they come to be related in the *Quartet*: 'Miss Crane, Miss Manners; Miss Manners, Miss Crane. At times there was a tendency to confuse them', thinks Barbie Batchelor, the missionary who once took over a teaching post from Edwina, and in some ways takes over her role in the narrative after her death (*TS* 62). Like the historical events which inspired them, both are reminders of the inevitable degradation of human nature which follows in the wake of imperial rule.

Why should it be the worst of the past which is remembered

so persistently? The best answer can be found in Jawaharlal Nehru's *The Discovery of India,* a book which he dedicated to his colleagues and fellow-prisoners at Ahmadnagar Fort between 9 August 1942 and 28 March 1945: 'So long as the connecting links and reminders are present, and the spirit behind those events survives and shows itself, that memory also will endure'.[5] In the *Raj Quartet,* Lady Manners too feels that 'it isn't the best we should remember'; the narrator continues for her: 'We must remember the worst because the worst is the lives we lead' (*DSc* 334).

This sounds like the troubled Scott of *The Corrida at San Feliu.* However, as the already large cast of characters introduced in *The Jewel in the Crown* widens, especially as it comes to include the members of the Kasim and Layton families, new bearers of hope as well as new victims appear.

The second novel of the *Quartet* is entitled *The Day of the Scorpion,* a reference to the idea that a threatened scorpion stings itself to death. Ultimately, this refers to the thrashing around of the Raj in its final death-throes. The narrative opens with the early-morning arrest of Mohammed Ali Kasim, a Muslim Congress Party member who, as ex-Chief Minister of Ranput, still feels some goodwill towards the British. Kasim's arrest is made under the same indefensible Defence of India rules as Hari's; it is also on the same day as Nehru's arrest: 9 August 1942. As Scott had intended, 'POLITICALLY THE QUARTET NOW OPENS OUT' (*MAM* 168). Followed through in the remaining two novels, the story of this high-principled man and his family is one of the Quartet's great tragedies – and inspirations. It is also the best answer to those who accuse Scott of 'foregrounding... Britishers' narratives at the expense of stories of Indians'.[6]

Kasim's affability ('I'm sorry they've dragged you out of bed', p. 11) at once marks him out as a very different sort of victim from the prickly and troubled Kumar. This is a man of refinement, maturity and vision. It is not to be expected, then, that he would accept the Governor of Ranput's offer to escape imprisonment by joining the British again: 'you only offer me a job. I am looking for a country' (p. 20), he says firmly. And this is despite the fact that his position as a Muslim puts him out on a limb in the largely Hindu Congress. As a prisoner in the Fort at

Premanagar, Kasim learns of the problems in Mayapore. His own predicament does not prevent him from sympathizing with British sufferings, and he writes a letter of condolence to Lady Manners, whose husband he had known and respected. Thus a bridge is made between the tragedies of *The Jewel in the Crown* and those that follow for Kasim himself.

For Kasim's problems are not only political: he is finally released after nearly three years of detention, only to learn that his elder son, Sayed, is awaiting court-martial on the charge of treason. Sayed, an officer with the British forces, had been persuaded by news of his father's incarceration to defect to the INA, whilst a prisoner of war in Kuala Lumpur. Despite his own mixed feelings about the British, and his dream of a free India, Kasim is quite unable to support what he sees as his son's breach of faith. Their confrontation in the last novel of the *Quartet, A Division of the Spoils,* is arranged by none other than Colonel Merrick, for while the cast of victims changes, the villain remains the same: Merrick is by now involved in preparations for the INA trials. The interview between father and son is deeply moving, because Kasim tries to coach Sayed in a line of defence for the court-martial, despite his own disappointment and disapproval. Sayed himself is almost reduced to tears by this, and even though his political disagreements with his father make him intransigent (after all, he is determined not to plead guilty), his affection and concern for him remain. Kasim is stung rather than pleased by his rebellious son's solicitude, even imputing a lack of sensitivity to him. But his last words to Sayed are 'Allah be with you' (*DSp* 478). Like the interview of Hari by Nigel Rowan in *The Day of the Scorpion,* this is one of the most dramatic episodes of the *Quartet.*

Scott has been praised for his handling of the intricate political factors involved in the INA issue; however, he has also been accused of bias in allowing Kasim (an Indian) to castigate his son for 'treachery' towards the British. But there were many Indians who viewed the INA with suspicion.[7] Moreover, it is the human element which is most impressive here. There is a dignity about Kasim which is largely missing in Kumar and in Scott's earlier heroes, who have been weak-willed and at times even unbalanced. Besides going against his own instincts as a father, Kasim knows that his refusal to speak out in support of

Sayed and the INA robs him of all possibilities of political clout: 'The electorate would say, Who is this man who won't defend even his own son?' (*DSp* 487). But he prefers to take the long view, even beyond his or his family's personal sufferings, that turncoats should not be the basis of India's future security.

Six months after Kasim's release from the Premanagar Fort, his wife had died. By then, his favourite son was already in custody. But there is worse to come. Finally, Kasim must pay a father's supreme sacrifice: his younger son Ahmed, an uncommitted but not insensitive young man, whose understanding and support Kasim has only just won, accompanies the Layton sisters, their aunt and little Edward Bingham on their journey to Ranpur from the princely state of Mirat after Merrick's funeral. Targeted as a Muslim with Congress connections, Ahmed gallantly offers himself to the rioting Hindus who stop their express train. Kasim had last been seen trying to write a letter to Gandhi (who did indeed wish to cooperate with the Muslims in Congress) in which he already admitted to being in 'low spirits' and struggling with uncertainties (*DSp* 495). Now, his dream of a unified India is completely shattered; and the sons for whom he had wanted it are both lost to him, one by political differences, the other by death. But his response to this ultimate tragedy, the responsibility for which is so firmly laid at the door of the British ('We just let him go. We all of us sat here and let him go', cries Sarah, *DSp* 644), is predictably brave. He is seen briefly by Perron at the end: 'An impressive man. Hiding his grief' (*DSp* 657).

Kasim's steadiness is as futile, ultimately, as Ahmed's single heroic gesture; and Scott has portrayed men who make such unproductive self-sacrifices before – Tom Gower in *The Alien Sky*, for instance, or Greystone in *The Chinese Love Pavilion*. But these two remain admirable, because they reveal a conviction completely lost to the author of *The Corrida at San Feliu* – that human beings have a 'moral sense' which is capable of withstanding or confronting great pressures and producing acts of true nobility (*DSp* 489). The Indian politician and his apolitical son do not, in the end, provide viable images of manliness in the modern world, but they are important all the same, for expressing their author's renewal of faith in human nature.

A more productive renewal of faith obtains in the case of Sarah Layton. The elder of two daughters born in Pankot to an army colonel, she stands to inherit all the values of the Raj, as well as of her education in England. Indeed, the eccentric Maharanee of Mirat expresses astonishment when Perron points her out as a 'charming girl' at her lavish party: 'I detest English girls', she cries, 'They are always so stupid and rude' (*DSp* 71). But Sarah is neither; Merrick immediately recognizes her as a more feminine version of the rather clumsy Daphne. From the start, she is seen as the 'rock on which the Layton family had come to rest' (*DSc* 135), and, like Daphne, she is only strengthened by the troubles she meets. When the obnoxious Major Clark seduces her, she is not diminished, but freed from her inhibitions: 'She's always had guts. Suddenly she has nerve', comments Nicky Paynton. 'It makes one wonder what happened to her in Calcutta' (*TS* 268). Even the anguish that her subsequent abortion causes her is a source of strength, for she endures it alone, annoyed at herself for even wanting a shoulder to cry on. As Mrs Paynton and her cronies notice, her 'nerve' also translates into an increasingly critical attitude towards the behaviour of the British in India, and eventually, like Daphne, she is able to love an Indian man – though she is never, she says, actually 'in love' with Ahmed (*DSp* 653).

Since the Laytons, as a family, dominate the last three volumes of the *Quartet* and become closely involved with everyone around them in the inbred world of British India, Sarah's role becomes more and more important. As noteworthy as her visit to Daphne's baby in *The Day of the Scorpion* is the fact that she is 'patient' and 'attentive' to Barbie Batchelor from the beginning to the end of *The Towers of Silence* (p. 29), the third novel of the *Quartet*. This alerts the reader to the elderly woman's significance here: continuing on from Edwina's, Barbie's is the voice of the (by and large) misguided missionary effort in India. The title of this novel is explained by the dying Barbie's fixation on the vultures which she sees from her hospital window at the end of the narrative. The birds are attracted to the dead bodies on the Parsees' funeral towers, and she is 'proud' of them (p. 422), looking to the end of a life which she now sees as wasted; and to the end of the Raj, in which all her faith has finally been eroded. *The Towers of Silence* ends with Barbie's death after a tonga accident, on the same day that the first atomic bomb was dropped in Japan. The crisis that so clearly looms now is one which Sarah is much better equipped to face than Barbie.

As other characters besides Barbie reveal themselves to her, Sarah becomes vital not only to the narrative process but also to its moral structure (and the two become increasingly difficult to separate). It is Sarah, for example, who discerns Teddie Bingham's shallowness, and Merrick's 'burden' of feelings about the Manners case (*DSc* 232). Her role becomes even more important in the *Quartet*'s concluding novel, with its self-explanatory title – *A Division of the Spoils*. Family duties continue to take up much of her energy; but the 'special kind of empathy' which she develops with Ahmed helps to prepare the reader for the previously rather irresponsible young man's last heroic act (p. 572); and her relationship with Perron, that 'breath of fresh air' very deliberately blown in at the end here (*MAM* 168), points clearly to the future. The pair had already made love once in Pankot, before Perron's demobilization. Now, returning to India as an academic in 1947, Perron is present during the final devastating episode of the *Quartet*, and joins her in offering water to the dying who have been taken off their train at Premanagar. Nothing is settled yet; indeed, the pair are separated immediately by the complicated family and political crises in which they are both caught up. Perron decides to return briefly to Mirat, where he will be able to tell Kasim, a kinsman of the Nawab's, of his son's heroism. For her part, Sarah must get back into the compartment where her now twice-widowed sister and other family members, soon to be dispossessed from their lives in India, are awaiting her. But before she climbs in, Perron kisses her goodbye; there seems to be light at the end of this gloomy tunnel after all.

It is clear that the subject of India will never be one of boredom or indifference to either of these responsible and unselfish young people. Rather, they are among those who represent the 'collective conscience' which gives history its 'moral drift' (*MAM* 57). There is the feeling that Sarah will continue to make her individual and healing contribution to the understanding of India by Perron's side – a feeling which is confirmed in *Staying On* by the news that the two did marry, and that Perron, now established as a Professor of Modern History in England, has continued to specialize in Indian history: one of his past students puts in a shadowy appearance in the later novel, on a visit to India to give some lectures and 'collect material for a thesis' (*SO* 93).

Through the Kasims and the Laytons, Barbie Batchelor and hundreds of other less important characters in the Raj *Quartet*, Scott works through the savage pattern of assault and counter-assault which is introduced in *The Jewel in the Crown*, widening the scale of the human tragedy which the end of the Raj had come to represent for him – and also sending out shoots of such hope into the future.

The narrative means by which Scott accomplishes this are extremely varied and complex, and very much in tune with his times. He summarized them thus later:

> Use of The Writer – sometimes called The Stranger or The Traveller (according to circumstances.)... Interviews, letters, extracts from works or accounts written or tape-recorded by THE CHARACTERS (who have been approached for information) PLUS THE WRITER'S OWN *RECONSTRUCTIONS*. (*MAM* 167)

The 'writer', then, is not exactly Scott, and not exactly omniscient – though given to dropping hints about the future. Nor is he really a character in his own right; unlike the female narrator in Ruth Prawer Jhabvala's *Heat and Dust* (1975), a later novel about the British in India in which past and present are also interlocked, he is not given any family connection to the characters whose experiences he sets out to investigate. Returning after 'an eighteen-year absence... to pin down the truth about Miss Crane, Miss Manners and young Kumar' (*JC* 101), his most obvious function is to facilitate the inclusion of a variety of viewpoints and modes of address. He gets access to those characters who are still living in India, like Lili Chatterjee, and to documents like the unpublished memoirs of Brigadier-General Reid; and he elicits comments on these and his other written materials from the deputy commissioner of the time, Robin White. Moreover, the 'writer' is shown some of Daphne's letters, and later her journals. In this way, he draws into the narrative the kind of materials which (like Lady Butterfield's tape-recording in *The Bender*) seem to belie the fictionality of the text, and relate it to the world of verifiable communications. But as the *Quartet* continues, he himself slides further into the background, only putting in an occasional appearance, as, for example, when he asks for the reader's cooperation in making 'the necessary imaginative readjustment' to see Teddie Bingham's life from his own point of view (*TS* 111). In *A Division of the Spoils*, his function is largely taken over by the dependably objective Perron, introduced at the beginning of the narrative as one who seeks 'opportunities to study in depth human behaviour during an interesting period of history' (p. 10); and (as for some of the affairs at Pankot) by Sarah.

Since the role of 'the writer' is not to mediate or collate but simply to present the characters' own words – a role which inevitably produces continual dislocations of time and vision – at first sight this is not one of the strategies which Scott uses to make the whole enormous fabric of the *Quartet* cohere. That task seems to be fulfilled instead by the narrative techniques demonstrated above: the continuities of history and its 'reconstructions'; and the way themes are carried through by characters who reappear (most importantly, Merrick) or are re-examined (most importantly, Hari), or take over from each other (most importantly, as Sarah does from Daphne). A sense of unity is further reinforced by numerous leitmotifs and symbols, like the echoes of the name Jallianwallah Bagh, or the fires in which both Edwina Crane and Teddie Bingham die. There is no mistaking Scott's intention here. He uses Merrick, for example, to note the similarities between Sarah and Daphne, and then again to point out the parallel between Edwina Crane's last gesture and Bingham's: 'sitting there [near the blazing jeep] with Teddie made it all seem to connect' (*DSc* 434).

In a sense, though, 'the writer' is more fundamental to the overall design of the *Quartet* than any of these literary 'tricks' (*MAM* 87). In general, as I have already suggested, his status as a kind of researcher works to disclaim the division of the recorded events from substantiated reality: what readers are invited to relive is presented as part of their own historical past. But on the other hand, the accounts of these events are various, casting doubt on their individual reliability. As in *The Corrida at San Feliu*, therefore, Scott first draws the reader into situations which are then (as he puts it himself, in familiar formalist terms) made 'available for decoding' (*MAM* 86).[8]

# 5

# The *Raj Quartet*: Themes

In view of Scott's chosen technique, questions about 'what the author has to say' seem especially hard to answer, even unfair. However, Scott himself felt that 'Nothing is worse for a novel than for the novelist to see all sides of a question and fail to support one' (*MAM* 57); and while he disliked the idea that a novel should have a 'moral purpose', he agreed that it may well have a 'moral effect' (*MAM* 78). Themes do emerge, then, and these eventually take the reader beyond matters of time and place, beyond history in fact, and produce their more profound implications.

Racial prejudice, which Scott saw as the main log that is 'damming the stream' of 'the moral drift of history' in our times (*MAM* 145), is a central concern throughout the *Quartet*. Scott himself was well aware of the dangers of dealing with such a sensitive and complicated issue.[1] But he was determined to tackle it head-on.

And head-on it had to be: a more rigorous observance of the racial boundary was one inevitable consequence of the 1857–9 Mutiny, and Scott sets his work in the very years when this boundary had grown hardest to cross.[2] The *man-bap* mentality was being eroded by resentment on both sides as the independence movement gained momentum; besides, Scott himself had realized at last that it only cloaked condescension, perhaps even (as Merrick puts it) 'a mixture of perverted sexuality and feudal arrogance' (*Dsc* 327). Not without some regret, he consigns it to the anachronistic Teddie Bingham in the *Raj Quartet*. When Teddie sacrifices his life in an effort to bring INA defectors back into the fold of their old regiment, there is still something heroic about the gesture; but on the whole it is made to seem foolhardy, if not actually foolish. Scott saw – and shows – that the embattled sense of racial superiority was hardening, now, into outright contempt.

The case of Harry Coomer/Hari Kumar is far more telling than that of Forster's Aziz in *A Passage to India*. It is appalling as well as ridiculous that a personable and intelligent young man like Hari should lose all value for the British as soon as he arrives in India, simply because of his colour. Here Scott's preoccupation with male identity finally and most effectively elides with his interest in cultural identity.[3] On the personal level, Hari's shock when his old schoolfriend Colin Lindsey cuts him dead at the cricket ground in Mayapore first plunges him into the drinking bout which brings him to Merrick's notice; then it turns him towards Daphne, the only English person who still responds to him as an equal. In other words, the one cruel rejection based on the one skin-deep distinction is what precipitates Hari's whole tragedy. On the wider human level, what happens to Hari has happened to a whole nation, which has, on the same basis, come to be perceived as humanly inferior. Merrick for his part takes much of his malignity from being the vehicle of this colonial contempt, and it is inextricably involved in his own downfall, too.

Prejudice, as Scott realized, is a 'many-headed dragon' (*MAM* 121), and for all his long-established hatred of it, he was brave enough to admit in a candid talk to the Commonwealth Countries' League in London in 1969 that he had to contend with it in himself. Tracing it to the same kind of experiences as 'the writer' has, when the sights (and smells) of India's struggling masses assail him on the road from Bombay to Mayapore, and referring to the notoriously anti-immigrant Conservative politician Enoch Powell, Scott confessed: 'India always did, still does and probably always will bring out the Enoch in me' (*MAM* 95). But the purpose of Scott's speech was not to condone such negative responses. On the contrary, he likened them to an 'unexploded bomb' whose mechanism must be studied in order to defuse it (*MAM* 95). What was needed, he knew, was the will to overcome them.

Among his characters, Daphne proves wonderfully courageous in this respect. The same girl who confesses to shuddering instinctively at the sight of Lili Chatterjee's servants after the rape, braves death itself to carry the child she is convinced is

Hari's. A similarly dramatic victory occurs in the case of Scott's other early heroine, Edwina Crane. At the beginning of her mission-school career, Edwina shrinks even from the Eurasian teacher Miss Williams; but she determines thenceforth to battle her fears, to 'promote the cause of human dignity and happiness' (*JC* 18), and to reach out the hand of encouragement and help. Her long battle is only fully won (too late, she fears) when she crawls painfully back to hold Mr Chaudhuri's hand at the side of the road after the assault. According to their individual opportunities other characters have their own limited successes – are able, for instance, to relate to their Indian staff in ways which go far beyond *man-bap* feudalism. Mabel Layton and Barbie Batchelor and their beloved Aziz at Rose Cottage are good examples here.

As for Scott himself, one sign of his own progress in eliminating traces of prejudice is the fact that, unlike Miss Williams and the many Eurasian women who precede her in his earlier novels, Daphne's own mixed-race daughter is not tainted or burdened by her Indian blood.[4] On the contrary, she is entirely lovely, and entirely at ease with herself and her surroundings – where, he adds hopefully, 'there is always the promise of a story continuing' (*JC* 516).

Continuing – but how? By the end of the *Quartet*, the type of fraught relationship which proved so disastrous for Daphne and Hari has been replaced by another kind, lower-key but more relaxed, represented by Sarah's bond with the Nawab of Mirat's shy daughter. This is a beginning, at least; though whether it will outlast the 'perfidy' of the British towards princely states like Mirat is not known (*MAM* 19). Scott, who had never had any patience with the 'disguising masks of nations' (Preface to *PS* 95), found the illusion that 'some of us stand on one bank and some on the opposite' harder to dispel than he had thought. But he shows, by the inwardness with which he portrays the sufferings of characters like Hari and the Kasims, as well as through the problems of those who become deeply involved with them, his utter conviction that it must be done; for, he knew, 'So long as we stand like that we are not living at all' (*JC* 156).

This is not the only 'discovery' to set against the feeling of dismay which accompanies the ending of the Raj for so many of

Scott's characters. Their dispossession has to be faced as something both inevitable and right.

When Scott first arrived in Bombay, he explained later to Indian audiences, the liberal-humanist idealism which had predisposed him to dislike the whole colonial set-up was shaken by the realization that 'power is exerted in different ways by individuals' (*MAM* 121). This is clearly reflected in the *Quartet*. Neither Brigadier-General Reid, nor Merrick with that 'permanent sneer in his eyes' (Lili Chatterjee's perception, *JC* 91), 'personifies' this Raj which to some extent earned Scott's sympathy.[5] Merrick, as a hands-on agent of the Raj who deals harshly first with activists and then with INA defectors (whose trials would soon become the *cause célèbre* of the freedom fighters), stands throughout only for the worst of it. Robin White, whom Daphne herself had liked, is given the authority to criticize both Reid and Merrick in *The Jewel in the Crown*. White is and was far more sympathetic towards the Indians than either, and without completely exonerating himself from blame in these matters, his comments damn Reid for his cruel onslaught against the rioters in Mayapore in August 1942, as well as showing that Merrick knowingly 'bent the rules' in his treatment of Hari and his fellow suspects (*JC* 380). In particular, White explains: 'The drama Reid and I played out was that of the conflict between Englishmen who liked and admired Indians and believed them capable of self-government, and Englishmen who disliked or feared or despised them' (*JC* 361). Scott's leaning was evidently towards the former, progressive type of colonialism which White himself represents.

Not that Scott had given up his initial, fundamentally anti-imperialist stance. When White blames a 'lack of synchronisation of . . . wishes' for the failure to hand over power graciously (*JC* 382), he is not expressing a charitable view of a situation which the British had no right to be in at all. Rather, he is expressing a real, pragmatic concern with the question of timing, a concern that India should not be left in a state of disunity and disorder. What Scott had indeed come to deplore was the way anti-imperialism was being used at home as a pretext for the British to cut their losses in India and evade their last obligations there. This he saw as hypocritical – as the cultural critic Edward Said would no doubt agree.[6] Had Perron's parochial Aunt Charlotte cited 'the ethical argument that colonialism was immoral' (*DSp* 242), she would only have been sharing in this hypocrisy. Yet there should be no mistake about it: although Scott is inevitably writing from a postcolonial standpoint, he does not simply rest on the comfortable assumption that 'the argument against imperialism as a political structure . . . no longer needs to be made';[7] such an argument is clearly implied and fully supported in the *Quartet*.

Scott makes his most basic criticisms of the Raj through a more dependable commentator than White – Barbie Batchelor, who reflects on her life's work as a missionary during her five years as Mabel Layton's companion in Rose Cottage, Pankot.

The process of Barbie's disenchantment with the Raj is traced in detail, up until the point where it renders the previously garrulous old woman literally speechless. What upsets her most is, naturally, the part that she herself has played in it. For she sees at last the enormity of undermining a nation's identity by trying to destroy its spiritual and cultural traditions. For instance, when she hears about Edwina Crane's ordeal, she is haunted first by the other missionary's dead Indian colleague, and then, more tellingly, by the memory of a pupil of hers who had coloured Jesus's face blue like Krishna's. Barbie remembers confiscating all the children's blue crayons, leaving them nothing with which to colour the sky. In her dream about the incident, the pupil wants her name called out in class, but neither Barbie nor the little girl herself can remember it. The 'unknown Indian' later appears to Barbie in other guises (*TS* 75), and the old woman's death at the end of the narrative, after the tonga accident, is nothing short of a blessed release from the burden of the distress which this figure causes her.

There is a good deal of compassion for Barbie, especially when she is rendered homeless after Mabel Layton's death; but it is clear that no amount of 'good intentions' could have saved her from her fate (*TS* 423). Such intentions are symbolized by the delicate butterflies worked into the lace which she is wearing as a veil when her tonga overturns. During this climactic episode, Barbie instinctively reaches forward to help the driver control his horse, which is under impossible pressure from the heavy trunk full of her past history on a downhill slope. As she does so, however, the lace which she had just taken from the trunk blinds both herself and the old man. The symbolism of the lace as well as the trunk is clear: sympathy for individuals like Robin White and Barbie should in no way be interpreted as tolerance of the oppressive and destructive system which they have inherited and in which they have become enmeshed.

Since Rowan had long ago noted that the Raj was by no means Perron's 'favourite animal' (*DSp* 291), the last word on Scott's view of it can be left to Sarah, who only despises herself for her 'brave little memsahib act' on the platform of Premanagar (*DSp* 654). Distress at leaving India to the dreadful mayhem of Partition was tempered only by the conviction that there was no justification for the old ideology and no place for its agents in the modern world – as well as by the hope of better relationships between countries, and individuals, in the longer term.

Class-consciousness aggravates many of the conflicts in Scott's earlier novels, particularly in the two set in England. The *Quartet* is no exception. Marginal figures in Raj society, like Edwina Crane and Barbie Batchelor, are granted insight into it precisely because they *are* marginal. And they are marginal partly because they are unattached women in a patriarchal hierarchy, partly because they are missionaries rather than administrators – and partly because of their relatively humble origins. Barbie, who comes from Camberwell, and whose mother did dressmaking to compensate for her father's gambling losses, has the humbler origins of the two. Although the colonial mentality itself is associated by Perron with the middle and lower classes rather than the upper class, the more aristocratic Rowan disagrees with him – and on the basis of the Raj society depicted here, he would appear to be right.

In particular, nearly all the important Englishmen in the *Quartet* (including not only these two themselves, but also the Layton men and Major Clark) are graduates of Chillingborough, the public school which had so unfitted Hari Kumar for life *as an Indian* in British India. It was such schools that had traditionally channelled their brightest and best into the upper echelons of the Raj; but, by inspiring their pupils to see the implementation of colonial policies as a manly calling, they had also, inevitably, filled them with notions of their own superiority. In effect, their privileged backgrounds predisposed these men to exactly that lack of any real understanding of India which the missionary women in the *Quartet* so deeply deplore: the very name which Scott gives his representative school provides a steely antonym for Jallianwallah Bagh, the scene of harsh confrontation with the 'natives' at Amritsar in 1919.

Nor is there any escape from the invidious effects of such a background. It is a historically accurate detail that Merrick should be an outsider to the large group of ex-Chillingburians in the *Raj Quartet*. Just as missionaries in India tended to come from lower down the social scale than the memsahibs, so the men who led the police force were likely to have had inferior schooling to those of Indian Civil Service administrators or officers in the prestigious Indian regiments.[8] But Merrick is no less of an imperialist for that, nor is he any more kindly disposed to the Indians who come under his authority. On the contrary, his efforts to compensate for his feelings of inferiority have even more dire results for them.

For the most part, then, it is only those who are not directly involved in operating 'the old imperial machinery' who can appreciate fully the antiquation of the hierarchy created by earlier generations of old Chillingburians and sustained by their wives (*DSp* 116).[9] It is Sarah's distinction in the Quartet that although she is very much a Layton herself, she recognizes it too; as she says later, of the 'damned bloody senseless mess' which it produced, 'it was our responsibility, our fault that after a hundred years or more it still existed' (*DSp* 653).

As noted in my introduction, Scott was quite happy to see himself as a 'social novelist'. Yet he would have been depressed to find the *Raj Quartet* remembered primarily as 'an exploration and interpretation of history, in novel form'.[10] He had insisted from the outset 'that he was not, and had no intention of becoming, a historical novelist'.[11] What gives this work, like his earlier ones, its fundamental dynamism and power is not its historical material but the 'dangerous geometrical arrangement of personalities' into which some of his main characters fall (*JC* 145), and it is by successfully challenging this arrangement that he expresses his ultimately positive theme about the human potential for good.

Merrick's ubiquity has already been noted: he is the one character who appears consistently throughout. Yet his own consciousness is never explored from within.[12] This is because his fair complexion and blue eyes mask 'a darkness of the mind and heart and flesh' (*JC* 165); he is the 'dark side' not only of the Raj, but, as Sarah perceives, of humanity itself (*DSc* 435). In this respect, Merrick is an additional and powerful argument against the validity of the colour divide: none of the Indian characters has this kind of darkness. Not, of course, that Scott makes it seem the preserve of the British alone, for it is hinted at in Pandit Baba, the teacher who incites Mayapore youth to acts of subversion, and it can be imputed to the hoodlums who rape Daphne, as well as to those involved in the final phase of Merrick's counter-victimization, and to those who ambush the train to Ranpur. Nevertheless, it is through Merrick that the *duende* gets its fullest and final say in Scott's work.

The most important of the vulnerable younger men who are affected by Merrick are Hari Kumar and Teddie Bingham, and of these, Hari is by far the more significant.

In *The Jewel in the Crown*, Scott has the unimpeachable and perspicacious (though now physically blind) Sister Ludmila tell 'the writer' about Merrick's first encounter with him. A figure inspired by Mother Theresa, Sister Ludmila used to tend the destitute in Mayapore. Six months *before* Daphne's rape, Hari had been brought to her sanctuary drunk, and was washing under the pump in the yard when Merrick called, looking for a wanted man. Merrick's own lowly background had put him at a disadvantage even in grammar school. Resentment at Kumar's superior accent and manner immediately exacerbated the older man's usual dislike of Indians; so, it seems, did the perverse attraction Hari unintentionally exerted on him. Sister Ludmila recalls this encounter as a destined meeting between someone who *looked* wholesomely manly but who 'smelt all wrong' (p. 138), and a youth who had lost his direction in life. And she maintains that by the end of the encounter Merrick had 'already chosen the twisted, tragic way' (p. 149).

Merrick's chip on his shoulder about his social and educational background is one factor in this choice. Much later in the *Quartet*, Perron articulates the other, more fundamental one: Merrick is a repressed homosexual, and abhors this part of himself; 'Self-punishment being out of the question' (*DSp* 333), he punishes instead those to whom he is attracted. It is as if for the first time Scott is able not only to see the 'geometry' but also to admit the source of this familiar configuration in his work.

Merrick's punishment of Hari is not simply physical: like some of Scott's earlier troubled male characters (Joe MacKendrick and Edward Thornhill, for instance), he sets about trying to appropriate the other man's woman. However, Daphne proves obstinate, and goes off after the rape to have her baby. Since it is not so much romantic rivalry that impels him as the prior fixation with Hari, his campaign against Hari continues. Having robbed him of his freedom, Merrick next tries to destroy his self-respect. That is why he has Hari caned repeatedly on the buttocks, and touches and taunts him sexually, in the jail. Hari's description of all this to Rowan surely owes something to T. E. Lawrence's confession of his humiliation by a Turkish officer in *The Seven Pillars of Wisdom* (Scott was fascinated by Lawrence). But there are differences – here, it is not the victim who feels gratification and later guilt, but the perpetrator.[13] Sarah can still sense the guilt.

This is not the worst that Merrick does. Hari's frank and generally composed interview with Rowan reveals that Merrick did not permanently break his spirit. But his other important victim actually dies. Merrick arrives in Captain Edward Arthur David Bingham's tent during a lull in the storm, much as Saxby is blown into Tom Brent's life in *The Chinese Love Pavilion* on the wings of one. Teddie's father had won a Military Cross as a major in the Muzzafirabad Guides, and this dedicated young officer stands even more completely than the public school educated Hari for everything which Merrick is not. He is also 'really rather good-looking', but (as the Pankot memsahibs describe him in their gossip) in a rather ambiguous way (*DSc* 135–6). Inevitably, Teddie soon feels the older man's personality impinging dangerously on his. Thus, behind the story of Merrick's heroic attempt to save Bingham in the jungle lies another fiction: as Merrick later confesses to Sarah, the hunt for INA defectors there was 'just a mess that he wouldn't have got into without me' (*DSc* 407). This time Merrick really does step into the other man's shoes. Not only does he marry Susan Bingham (so recently née Layton), but he also becomes the stepfather of Teddie's posthumous child Edward, whom he sets out to bring up in his own image as a 'little Pathan' (*DSp* 555).

Much is involved in this (at first sight) surprising match. If Merrick's proposal to Susan is partly prompted by the fact that she had been Teddie's wife, it is also, as Susan's father himself realizes, a bid to gain a foothold in the highest social echelons of the Raj. But there is another possibility, too. Susan is the Layton most closely associated with the symbolism of the suicidal scorpion: born under the sign of Scorpio, she had reacted to Teddie's death by setting their new-born infant in a ring of flames, as she had once seen a *mali* (gardener) set a scorpion. Although she reasoned that she was freeing her child from the miseries of this world, the image was a cruel one. By marrying such a woman, Merrick is doing more than stepping into Teddie's shoes; consciously or unconsciously, he is trying to strengthen the element in the Layton family which had not 'gone soft' like Colonel Layton and Teddy (*DSp* 230). Among such considerations, one, of course, is missing. There is never any suggestion that he loves Susan. Described once by Sarah as being 'outside in the cold' (*DSc* 431), Merrick suffers more than any of the other disturbed young men in Scott's novels from the 'handicap at love' referred to in my introduction.

Merrick's other questionable actions in the *Quartet* only confirm the pattern established by his treatment of Hari. As part of his vendetta against the INA, for instance, Merrick cruelly humiliates an Indian defector whose father had once been decorated for bravery, and who had probably been coerced into his defection. Unable to detach himself spiritually from the situation as Hari had done, Havildar Muzzafir Khan hangs himself in the prison. Thus Hari who is also Harry is Teddy as well, and Khan, and anyone else (whether Indian or British) who has to field Merrick's 'merciless succession of contemptuous deliveries' (*DSp* 357). Scott has used this kind of incremental repetition before, most noticeably in *The Corrida at San Feliu*; in the *Quartet*, too, it suggests the force of the *duende* in human life, building up again and again, and continually seeking new objects on which to release its fury.

Exactly because there is a strong sense that he is compelled to act as he does, Merrick is no stage villain, but a fully convincing character.[14] Representing the 'arcane side' of human nature

(*DSc* 435), which Scott recognized in himself and which at once appalled and fascinated him with its explosive mixture of envy, contempt, sexual need and self-hatred, he often dominates the action and other characters' thoughts, and even gets opportunities to appeal to the reader's sympathy. In an indirect confession to Sarah he admits human fallibility, and passes some of the responsibility to the Raj for giving it rein: 'I sometimes think that if I'd done something terribly wrong the rubber stamp would have endorsed it' (*DSc* 234). This is perhaps the closest Scott himself comes to identifying Merrick with the Raj; but at the same time Merrick's official role sets the limit to his powers. For the Nawab's canny chief minister, Count Bronowsky, puts it to Perron that in the end Merrick invited his own nemesis: after finally yielding to his homosexual impulse with an Indian boy, the Count surmises, Merrick would have found his contempt for the subject race, and the whole career which was based on it, called into question, and would have been unable to go on living with himself.

All this is rather different from what happens to Saxby, Merrick's most significant precursor in Scott's earlier novels. Saxby dies unreclaimed and still in possession of a devotee. But Scott is making his discoveries now, freeing his characters (and himself?) from such malign and destructive energies. Against Merrick he sets not only some horrified part of the character's own self, but also a whole panoply of protagonists who suggest what else human beings have it in them to be. Apart from Daphne and Sarah, these fall into two distinct groups – older women who (rather like Mrs Moore in Forster's *A Passage to India*)[15] have achieved wisdom; and younger men who are more resistant to Merrick's extraordinary influence.

Of the former, Mabel Layton, who has withdrawn from Pankot society into her deafness and the sanctity of her rose garden, is closest to Mrs Moore. As she says to Barbie in the Officers' Mess of the Pankot Rifles, where the silver donated by her first husband is part of the chilly display of Raj splendours, 'I can't even be angry' (*TS* 210). But Lady Manners is a more active version of the type. She puts into play the understanding she has gained: she gives shelter to her niece, raises her child, and takes steps to remove the uncertainty surrounding Parvati's parentage. Although she believes Hari to be beyond 'either our incriminations or our help' (*JC* 506), her request for his re-examination nevertheless results in his release from jail. One of the last things noted about her is that 'Nowadays the old lady has almost more Indian friends than she has British' (*DSp* 186).

As for the latter type, the stronger young men, these are where Scott has been painfully heading for some time with characters like Ian Canning in *A Male Child*.

Guy Perron is the best example here. He is the one person who, until just before the end, regularly refers to Hari as Harry Coomer: unlike Colin Lindsey, he does not consider the ex-Chillingburian to be 'invisible' simply because they are all in India now (*DSc* 279). After making love to Sarah, Perron even dreams of being in Hari's place on the night of the rape, for he too has overstepped his mark with a woman: Sarah, though a sergeant like himself (in the Woman's Auxiliary Corps), is after all a colonel's daughter. There are even signs that Perron has become yet another of Merrick's targets. The difference is that he cannot be so easily intimidated. This is not just a matter of his circumstances – the aunt who can pull strings, the available niche in academe. Perron can see right through the other man. Most usefully, he recognizes Merrick's eager adoption of received social values. Here, he draws on Emerson, whom Barbie admires too, taking from his essay 'Self-Reliance' the idea that 'Society is a wave' in which weaker individuals of this kind soon drown. In claiming that he and Rowan are exceptions to the rule, Perron also (apparently unwittingly) echoes Emerson's belief in the superiority and inviolability of certain people (*DSp* 228–9). These are the ones who *are* self-reliant – who know who they are, and act on that knowledge.

Aware of deriving a sense of security from his own social background, and referring cynically to the sheltered career on which he has already embarked by the end of the *Quartet*, Perron is by no means a conventional hero. But to such a man as this, who does know himself, who understands others and can judge them impartially, and who can commit himself to a woman on these sound bases, neither the crises of history nor a man like Merrick can pose any real threat.

The movement of the *Quartet* has been described as circular;[16] it certainly deals with the cycle of 'creation, preservation and destruction' symbolized by Siva's dance and inscribed by the British Raj (*JC* 157). But Scott ends the *Quartet* with a passage from the fictional Urdu poet Gaffur, which suggests many possibilities of progress:

> ...even you, Gaffur, can imagine
> In this darkening landscape
> The bowman lovingly choosing his arrow,
> The hawk outpacing the cheetah,
> (The fountain splashing lazily in the courtyard),
> The girl running with the deer.

Understandably, there is an elegiac feel about the general 'landscape' here, as the last curtains of the Raj, and of this whole extraordinary work, come down together. But, as Scott pointed out himself, 'ALL THE LAST LINES REFER TO OTHER IMAGERY' (*MAM* 169), and they do so in a very positive way.

The 'bowman' of course recalls Hari in his difficult role as Philoctetes. But this is less Hari the victim than Hari the hero – the archer who is 'needed... after all' (*DSp* 606), and exercises his skill 'lovingly' again after his cure.[17] Taking the long view, it is thanks to the kind of nostalgia with which Hari writes of his English past in the *Ranpur Gazette* that the relations between postcolonial India and England have been more affectionate than bitter. The cheetah mentioned in the following line brings to mind Susan's two unmanageable puppies called Panther, the first of which turned vicious during her breakdown, 'wreaking havoc' in the rose garden (*TS* 350).[18] Here, however, the cheetah is outpaced by a hawk – which at once evokes Ahmed's intelligent Mumtaz, the bird whose performance thrilled Sarah at Mirat. The well-trained mind, it seems, is capable of controlling undisciplined and dangerous impulses. The fountain which Gaffur depicts next also brings back a scene in Mirat. Perron had watched Sarah put her arm round the Nawab's daughter, who was sitting by the fountain in the sunlit palace courtyard, and then walk up to the terrace with her. Since Perron was in love with Sarah by then, the scene suggested the possibility not only of close personal bonds across the racial and political divide, but also of romantic attachment between man and woman. And finally, the girl 'running with the deer' evokes not so much Daphne as her graceful daughter, who, far from hurrying away from some calamity, is hastening to her music lessons, and to a future full of promise.

When Daphne puts on her hated glasses to examine Sister Ludmila's carving of the dancing Siva, she sees that he has one foot firmly on an ugly dwarf. This represents Siva's conquest of the ego with its 'demoniac qualities' which destroys man's peace of mind by tempting him with its desires.[19] As far as the *Quartet*'s spiritual dimension is concerned, the image of the hawk outpacing the cheetah is the most significant of those discussed above, since it represents just this kind of victory, and one which Scott has long been wanting to celebrate. Another piece of Emerson remembered by Perron expresses it more explicitly. It concludes: '*If there be virtue, all the vices are known as such; they confess and flee*' (*DSp* 368). Fittingly (for Perron is with Sarah when he recalls this passage, and feels that she has it in mind as well), this comes from the essay on 'Love', in which the great American Transcendentalist writes of the love of man and woman as an enabling force, and part of the progress of the soul towards its own perfection.

# 6

# *Staying On* – and Afterwards

'It is necessary finally', he said, 'to think what life is all about'.

'Exactly', Mr Bhoolabhoy said, suddenly having a vision of Mrs Bhoolabhoy who – at this very moment – would be checking Management's accounts. (*SO* 128)

The information about Sarah's marriage to Perron is quite incidental to *Staying On*, Scott's next and last novel. He was not trying to wind up the plot of the *Quartet* here, nor was he simply indulging his penchant for recycling names or having one or two figures from an earlier novel put in brief reappearances.[1] Rather, *Staying On* represents the 'going back' which William Conway in *The Birds of Paradise* sees as a kind of duty, a duty to confirm the past which has been recreated in the mind, and to validate what was found in it. *Staying On* is a splendid achievement in its own right, and was immediately recognized as such; but, especially in view of Scott's early training, it can also be seen as a final audit. It is one in which the novelist succeeds in producing both acceptance and a degree of closure.

In the *Raj Quartet*, the Smalleys are just what they sound – small figures who almost disappear in a vast canvas. Scott puts them on a par with his ubiquitous Smith's Hotels when he introduces them in *The Towers of Silence*: 'Most stations had their Smalleys... slight bores but very useful' (51–2). Indeed, the nondescript and childless army couple, Major (later Colonel) 'Tusker' Smalley and his not quite pukka wife Lucy, do live in rooms in a Smith's Hotel in Pankot, during the whole period covered by the *Quartet*.

When Scott takes them up again in *Staying On,* nothing has changed for the better. Tusker has moved from Pankot to a company job in Bombay and back again to Smith's, with his ineffectually protesting wife in tow, the only differences to their living arrangements being that they now have a yearly tenancy of the hotel's annexe, otherwise known as The Lodge, and that the whole place, overshadowed by the new and majestic Shiraz right opposite, is shabbier and more run down than ever. The last of Pankot's retired ex-colonials, they themselves are 'people in shadow' (p. 40): the faithful Ibrahim puts layers of polish on Lucy's shoes and attends assiduously to her modest wardrobe of twinsets and so forth, but the 'treacherous sunlight' shows up her worn handbag cruelly at the Menektaras' Holi party (p. 176). Colonel Menektara and his wife are the new occupants of Rose Cottage, and they represent the smart set of Indians who have replaced the Laytons and their ilk in Pankot. To this social scene, the Smalleys are even more peripheral than they used to be to the inner circle of Raj society. Worst of all, their future is in the hands of the gross and unscrupulous Lila Bhoolabhoy, the present owner of Smith's, a Dickensian tartar who dominates her more kindly disposed husband Francis (Frank, or Franky when in his wife's good books) even more than Tusker dominates his diminutive wife. The Smalleys' stature, never high, has shrunk almost to nothing.

That the narrative opens with the announcement of Tusker's death from a second heart attack hardly raises the reader's hopes. Seen in flashback, the events of the plot work forwards to it again inexorably. From the start, it is linked to the Letter (purposefully capitalized) which Lila Bhoolabhoy forces Frank to send Tusker; but the contents are not divulged until the penultimate chapter, by which time they have all the weight of a death sentence: 'Ownership' is selling out to a consortium, and the Smalleys (like Barbie in the *Raj Quartet,* and like the long-suffering Ibrahim here, as well) are to 'get the push' (p. 64). It is while rushing furiously from The Lodge to confront her with this letter that Tusker collapses among the red canna lilies.

Added to this disaster which hangs over the whole narrative are the cumulative disappointments of several lifetimes, even of an era, evoked through Scott's characteristic mix of narrative devices – amongst others, Lucy's reminiscences and her correspondence with Sarah Perron (née Layton), and Tusker's two written notes, one about his unenterprising career, and the other about the dismal financial situation in which his death will leave Lucy. Lucy's 'rather... sad life' is Scott's main focus here p. 82), and it is easy enough for both Lucy and the reader to dwell on her missed chances, her let-downs, and the petty cruelties she has experienced, both in childhood and after being yoked to the undemonstrative Tusker. But others have their regrets, too: Ibrahim thinks wistfully of 'the days of the *raj*... when the servants were treated as members of the family' (p. 30), and Frank is disturbed by the rumblings of a guilty conscience about his lust for Hot Chichanya at the Go-Go Inn, not to mention the part he must play in ousting the Smalleys. It seems apt, then, that when the Anglo-Catholic Father Sebastian comes to preach for the first time at St John's in Pankot, he should choose a particularly gloomy text from Ecclesiastes 2: 17–19 ('Therefore I hated life...').

Yet Tusker's death is juxtaposed not only with the brilliant lilies, but also (in the very first sentence) with the information that Lucy is getting a blue rinse at the Seraglio Room of the Shiraz at the time. There is a vitality here which flies in the face of the uncompromising movement from disillusion to death. This lifts the narrative even from its lowest points into moments of high comedy. Tusker, for example, suffers his first heart attack while perching on his old-fashioned throne of a toilet; and Ibrahim is called to help just when approaching climax with the Bhoolabhoys' servant Minnie. 'Coming, Memsahib!' he cries out loyally, provoking the metafictional aside: 'The overstatement of the week' (p. 44). More important than the laughter, though, is the quiet celebration of those elements which redeem the Smalleys' 'little lives' and make them, after all, worth the living.

Admittedly, love is not something that springs to mind in connection with this couple. But it is the most important of these elements. The romance which blossomed in 1930, when Tusker first stepped into the Chancery Lane office where Lucy was a secretary, has been submerged by a tide of aggravations and frustrations, but it has not died. It resurfaces at critical moments in their lives. One such occasion, to which so much of Scott's whole *oeuvre* has tended, is the lowering of the Union Jack on Independence Day, on the parade ground at Pankot. Tusker takes his wife's hand, sharing the bitter-sweet moment with her without needing the words which he was never brought up to say. A much more recent, more intensely private moment is when Lucy comforts Tusker in his distress over the neglect of his lawn at The Lodge. 'You mustn't be upset', cries Lucy: 'who cares whether it is cut or not so long as it is not cut for both of us, and so long as we're together?' (p. 53). Still, Lucy now puts into action a secret plot to comfort Tusker by finding (and funding) a substitute for the gardener sacked by 'Ownership'. It is the less surprising, then, that Tusker's letter of accounts for Lucy should contain the words: 'You've been a good woman to me, Luce. Sorry I've not made it clear I think so' (p. 232), and that he should shorten her name to point up its association with the Latin *lucere*, to shine. The significance of this is lost on Lucy, but the sentiment is not: she keeps the letter under her pillow that night (the last night of Tusker's life) like a young girl with a *billet-doux*. Sad, yes, and also rather ridiculous; but her own feelings here are unequivocal: 'Peace enveloped her' (p. 233).

And there have been other satisfactions. Like so many of Scott's characters, both Lucy and Tusker have taken a quiet pride in their work. Tusker admits to having enjoyed his apparently dull desk jobs, enjoyed 'paper, working things out on it, arranging things with it' (p. 85); Lucy defends the elegance and efficiency of the Pitman's shorthand which has made her, over the years, 'in demand on every woman's committee that was going' (p. 87). She has not had the full life she yearned for, it is true; her talent for drama, for instance, finds an outlet only in her interior monologues or private mutterings, her useless tirades against Tusker, or her display of unconcern when he collapses at the Menektaras'. But thanks to her serviceable skill, she has not had the empty life which drove someone like Sarah's mother Mildred Layton to drink and adultery.

Moreover, both the Smalleys have enjoyed their place of work – not British India, but India itself. The happiest time in their marriage was when Tusker worked in the princely state of Mudpore, earning his nickname not from his regimental insignia so much as from his dealings with the Maharajah's elephants – whose behaviour improved when he increased their feeding allowance. Lucy had no say in the matter of 'staying on', and she faces a lonely future when Tusker dies, but it is extremely doubtful whether she would have been any better off or have any better prospects in 'some place like bloody Stevenage' (p. 213). She recognizes (and tells Father Sebastian at the end) that Tusker has been 'happy here' (p. 250), and when she herself yearns to go 'home' after Tusker's death (p. 255), she is not using the word as earlier memsahibs have used it: as with Srinivas, the elderly Indian immigrant in Kamala Markandaya's *The Nowhere Man* (1972), life in another land has effectively cut her off from her own country of origin. The 'home' she means is death, where she can be reunited with her exasperating but indispensable husband.

'Staying on' acquires a different and deeper meaning at this point. It is easy to overlook the spiritual dimension of the narrative, with its often scatological and ribald humour. But Lucy is never made fun of. Her composure and dignity never fail her in public, and while they hide her sorrows they reveal her strength too. The source of this strength is partly the determination to retain her dignity, but partly, too, a genuine selflessness. Despite Tusker's death, for instance, Mr Turner's visit is not to be postponed: he is bringing a gift from Susan and Sarah to Minnie, who is none other than the ayah who had once looked after Susan and Teddie's baby: 'it would be a big thing in Minnie's life to find herself remembered as the little ayah', Lucy feels, and 'One could not think only of oneself' (pp. 253–4). This selflessness is connected with the way Lucy's modesty and attentiveness is felt by Frank (himself a lay-preacher there) to grace St John's C. of E. Church in Pankot, and give meaning to the services. She feels desperate on the night of Tusker's death, but it is clear that she will endure whatever has to be endured with characteristic fortitude.

The hymn chosen on Father Sebastian's first visit to St John's is that rousing old favourite 'Onward, Christian Soldiers', and the penultimate verse is quoted here. It provides a clear response to the gloom of the Father's text from Ecclesiastes – and to Scott's own picture of a postcolonial India dominated not only by the sophisticated Menektaras (who have restored Mabel Layton's rose garden) but also, less happily, by entrepreneurs like Lila Bhoolabhoy:

Crowns and thrones may perish,
  Kingdoms rise and wane,
But the church of Jesus
  Constant will remain;
Gates of Hell can never
  'Gainst the Church prevail;
We have Christ's own promise,
  And that cannot fail.

(131)

Scott, whose first published work, *I, Gerontius*, was a poem in search of religious faith, but whose missionaries in the *Raj Quartet* suffer torments of doubt and despair, seems to be offering some spiritual certainty at last. Like Eliot, the writer whom he considered to have been 'perhaps the greatest literary influence on [his] life' (*MAM* 119), he clothes it in the rituals of Anglo-Catholic Christianity, for the new priest not only styles himself 'Father' but conducts his services on distinctly 'popish' lines. But Father Sebastian is also much involved with the ecumenical movement, and in a Pankot where the Hindu fertility festival of Holi is as much a cause for celebration as Easter, there is no sense of the religious exclusiveness which had so troubled Barbie in *The Towers of Silence*. On the contrary, the breath of hope here is not only for the Smalleys, who take to Father Sebastian at once, but also for the relationship of East and West – a hope already epitomized by the strange but inspiring mixture of elements in his services, where even laughter has a place, and which brings a smile even to Lucy's lined face.

The tonga for which Lucy had been waiting with Tusker, and for which she is left waiting alone at the end, reminds the reader of the apotheosis which Barbie looks for and feels she has found when her tonga begins to career downhill in the last chapter of *The Towers of Silence*. It also begs comparison with the chariot in Patrick White's *Riders in the Chariot* (1961), where the Australian novelist gives his principal characters their own individual intimations of their spiritual conveyance; in White's novel, it is clear that what matters is not the shape which these intimations take, but the 'Bit of life' which informs them (*SO* 184).

Positive readings of the *Raj Quartet* and *Staying On* are supported by the change which is known to have come over

Scott during the last period of his life: he was at peace with himself at last.[2] It was not simply that the recognition and financial rewards which came with the Booker Prize lifted old burdens of resentment and insecurity. The process of reconciliation with his family started before *Staying On* was even published. An early sign of it was his collaboration with his younger daughter, Sally, on a poignant version of *Cinderella*. Published posthumously, this was entitled prophetically *After the Funeral* (1979) – the funeral being that of Cinderella's mother, who has only just died when the story opens. As the youngest daughter of an impoverished baron, Scott's Cinderella never does go to the ball; but she is not embittered by this or her earlier disappointments. '. . . warmed by work and expectation' (p. 6), she finds that it is enough simply to hear the music, see 'the pictures in the fire', and sense the presence of love (p. 19).

Scott was luckier than his own Cinderella: he tasted at least the first fruits of his success, looking forward to the filming of *Staying On*, and having grounds for hope that it would be followed by an adaptation of the *Raj Quartet*, as indeed it was. He already had some assurance, too, that he would be fortunate in his first critics, two of the most admiring of whom he had met in America. K. Bhaskara Rao, whose book was published only two years after Scott's death, goes so far as to call the *Quartet* 'the Anglo-Indian *War and Peace*';[3] Francine Weinbaum, then a graduate student to whom Scott had been particularly forthcoming, also notes its Tolstoyan dimensions in a sympathetic study which finally came out in 1992.[4] Among the more established critics who have written appreciatively on Scott, Mollie Mahood talks only a little more cautiously of his 'Tolstoyan aspirations', going on to argue forcefully for the 'magnitude' of his achievement.[5]

In fact, it does Scott no real service to be compared to Tolstoy. His effort to present all sides of any given situation (whether an accident in jungle training or the collapse of an ideology) robs him of the magisterial moral authority of the Russian novelist, introducing instead a very modern note of enquiry and debate. This relates the *Raj Quartet* much more closely to the novel sequences of his contemporaries, Doris Lessing (*Children of Violence*, 1952–1969) and Lawrence Durrell (*The Alexandria Quartet*, 1957–60), which explore a variety of personal, literary and political issues in a highly self-conscious way.[6] Inevitably, as Durrell's character Pursewarden suggests, narratives like these 'raise in human terms the problems of causality and indeterminacy';[7] and Scott's often troubled awareness of this also robs him of the light touch of, say, R. K. Narayan, or the exuberance of more characteristically capacious Indian writers in English with whom he might be compared – G. V. Desani, for instance, or Raja Rao, or Rushdie.

But Paul Scott, like any other important writer, deserves to be recognized first and foremost for his own distinctive voice and his own distinctive achievement.

The voice is the one he himself began to recognize even as a young apprentice writer in Southgate: unmistakably English, marked with the uneasiness and self-consciousness of a writer shaped by middle-England, but never comfortable with it. When he was jolted out of this confinement by exposure to a totally different culture, he sifted the experience to see what good would accrue from it, for himself as a writer, and for the generations of others who had shared the experience. In this respect he is indeed closest to Forster, though the fact that the *Raj Quartet* postdates *A Passage to India* by several decades gives him a tremendous edge: as Michael Gorra points out, 'The great English novel about imperialism could not be written until after empire was gone'.[8] But what is even more compelling about Scott's voice, from a literary point of view, is the note of the *duende* in it, the edge of desperation as the emotionally compromised self is brought to confront this larger world in narratives of increasing complexity. That he allows the *duende* to have its say is one of Scott's biggest strengths, and Merrick in particular is all the more memorable for appearing during a period of literary history which, as Iris Murdoch has pointed out, is (for all its preoccupation with violence) strangely short on 'convincing pictures of evil'.[9]

Nevertheless, the *duende* does not by any means have the last word in Scott's work. Earlier critics have focused on this author's sense of lost ideals ('Paul Scott's novels are about the loss of Paradise')[10] and frustrated desires (what Weinbaum calls 'the repression of instinct and its unavoidable consequences');[11] but he should not be seen as a casualty of either postwar, post-empire disillusion, or his own inner conflicts. Nor does he use postmodern narrative strategies simply to throw his reader 'off balance'.[12] His purpose was always to involve his readers more actively in the narrative, to make them 'see, share and contribute to the building of' a new version of reality (*MAM* 87). In the last analysis, neither the scale and complexity of the *Raj Quartet* nor exceptional characters like Saxby and Merrick constitute Scott's greatest achievement. What is most inspiring about his work is the way this version of reality evolves, as his uneasy earlier heroes are replaced, in the confrontation mentioned above, by much stauncher characters like Daphne Manners, Mohammed Ali Kasim and Lucy Smalley.

The process is undoubtedly a painful one, involving as it does the honest disclosure and eventual crushing of those prejudices, misplaced loyalties, and sexual compulsions which, Scott felt, can only warp and impede human relationships, whether between men, men and women, or indeed whole countries. This might perhaps become the aim of the whole postcolonial enterprise, as it moves forward from its anticolonial stance. As for postmodernism, in its widest definition, this connotes not a search for identity, resolution and hope, but an acceptance, wry or even celebratory, of things as they are – in flux, uncertain, unpredictable. History is not so much open to reinterpretation, and in that sense rewritable, as irrelevant here. And there is something of all this in Scott's last novel, too. 'I love life', he told his friend Roland Gant simply and unreservedly just a few days before his death (*AF* xiii). Scott has never held out the promise of easy answers and instant rewards; there is no facile optimism in his work; but, like Daphne herself, he was 'strangely of good heart' at the end of it all. And through the laughter of *Staying On*, he invites his readers to be (in every sense) 'of good heart' too.

# Notes

## INTRODUCTION

1. Salman Rushdie, 'Outside the Whale', *American Film*, 10 (January 1985), 70.
2. Neil Lazarus, *Resistance in Postcolonial African Fiction* (New Haven: Yale University Press, 1990), 5.
3. Michael Gorra, *After Empire: Scott, Naipaul, Rushdie* (Chicago: University of Chicago Press, 1997), 59.
4. See especially 'The Architecture of the Arts: The Novel', *My Appointment with the Muse*, 71–89.
5. Sidney M. Jourard, 'Some Lethal Aspects of the Male Role', in Joseph H. Pleck and Jack Sawyer (eds.), *Men and Masculinity* (Englewood Cliffs, NJ: Prentice-Hall, 1974), 27.

## CHAPTER 1. A DIVIDED LIFE

1. An event narrated to Jean G. Zorn, who interviewed him for the *New York Times Book Review*, 21 August 1977, 37. Scott came to believe more and more in 'the influence of the mysterious genes' (*MAM* 45).
2. Full details of these relationships may be found in Hilary Spurling's *Paul Scott: A Life* (London: Pimlico, 1991), 63–78.
3. For a discussion of Scott's problems in early 1941, see Spurling, *Paul Scott*, 92–101. Later, Spurling maintains that, for Scott, 'marriage had been a purifying and protective measure' (p. 131).
4. R. C. Majumdar, H. C. Raychaudhuri and Kalikinkar Datta, *An Advanced History of India*, 4th edn. (Madras, Bombay, Calcutta, Delhi: Macmillan India, 1978), 977.
5. For details of Scott's movements in India, see Robin Moore, *Paul Scott's Raj* (London: Heinemann, 1990), 14–20.
6. Of the former, Malcolm Muggeridge wrote, 'we who actually lived under the Raj, and think we know what it was really like, look

askance at efforts...to bring it back to life' (review of *Staying On* in *New York Times Book Review*, 21 August 1977, 36). As explained in my introduction, Rushdie includes Scott in his impassioned diatribe against what he sees as 'British nostalgia for the lost hour of their precedence' and 'the rise of Raj revisionism' (pp. 70, 72).

7. For details of the screen adaptation of the *Raj Quartet* and its reception, see George W. Brandt, '*The Jewel in the Crown* (Paul Scott – Ken Taylor). The Literary Serial; or the Art of Adaptation', in Brandt (ed.), *British Television Drama in the 1980s* (Cambridge: Cambridge University Press, 1993), 196–213.

## CHAPTER 2. NOVELS OF THE FIFTIES

1. 'English men and women are, as it were, members of one great family, aliens under one sky' (Maud Diver, *The Englishwoman in India*, London: Blackwood, 1909, 33).
2. See for example Alun Lewis's fine poem, 'The Jungle'. Lewis went out on the Athlone Castle a few months before Scott, and trained in the same area of India. See *Selected Poems of Alun Lewis*, ed. Jeremy Hooker and Gweno Lewis (London: Unwin, 1981).
3. Bernard Gutteridge, then a major in Burma, expressed very similar feelings in his poem 'Namsaw. The C. O.', *Traveller's Eye* (London: Routledge, 1947).
4. Scott's original ending leaves Craig holding the dead cadet's hand – a gesture to be made use of later, when Edwina Crane holds her dead colleague's hand (*JC* 66). This ending is printed in Bruce J. Degi, 'Paul Scott's Indian Army: *The Mark of the Warrior* and *The Raj Quartet*', CLIO 18:1 (1988), 43–4.
5. Marc Feigin Fasteau, *The Male Machine* (New York: McGraw-Hill, 1974), 157. Cf., more recently, George L. Mosse's discussion of the warrior as 'a climax to the concept of manliness inherent in much of the construction of modern masculinity' (*The Image of Man: The Creation of Modern Masculinity*, Oxford: Oxford University Press, 1996, 107).
6. However, this was a common experience and exactly what was intended: see Lewis's description of being pushed to the limit on a similar exercise in *In the Green Tree* (London: Allen and Unwin, 1948), 42.
7. Significantly, Scott acknowledged that Esther was based on Penny Scott. See Spurling, *Paul Scott*, 216.

## CHAPTER 3. NOVELS OF THE EARLY SIXTIES

1. David Lodge, *Working with Structuralism: Essays and Reviews on Nineteenth- and Twentieth-Century Literature* (London: Ark Paperbacks, 1986), 14.
2. Lacan uses the term 'other' for various purposes. Referred to here is what he calls the 'paternal metaphor', which plays a vital part in normal psychic functioning. See Madan Sarup, *Jacques Lacan* (London: Harvester Wheatsheaf, 1992), 108–10.
3. Rao, K. Bhaskara, *Paul Scott* (Boston: Twayne, 1980), 25.
4. Spurling, *Paul Scott*, 266.

## CHAPTER 4. THE *RAJ QUARTET*: A STUDY IN NARRATIVE

1. An Indian view of the massacre is given in V. S. Savarkar's *Indian War of Independence* (Bombay: Phoenix, 1947); more details about it, and the questions it raises, are given in P. J. O. Taylor's *A Star Shall Fall: India 1857* (New Delhi: Indus, 1993), 114–21. Scott's shifting approaches allow him to reflect accurately the controversies surrounding this affair.
2. The important buildings in the *Raj Quartet* encapsulate the history of their occupants and their times, and are a subject for study in themselves. Important examples are Lili Chatterjee's MacGregor House and (later) the Laytons' 'squat, functional and aggressive' Rose Cottage in Pankot (*DSp* 297).
3. For Pathans as marauders, see Majumdar, Raychaudhuri and Datta, 718–19; on their sexual reputation, see Rao, *Paul Scott*, 152, n. 8. NB, Merrick's behaviour is not as extraordinary as it sounds: political agents acquired 'a chameleon-like ability to mix with warring tribesmen on the North-West Frontier' (Charles Allen, *Raj: A Scrapbook of British India*, 1877–1947, London: André Deutsch, 1977, 70, 126). The scrapbook also shows that the English enjoyed dressing up in such ways!
4. Majumdar, Raychaudhuri and Datta, *An Advanced History of India*, 971. Again, there were conflicting accounts of this, with General Dyer himself changing his ground between his first and second statements about it. See Philip Mason's *The Men Who Ruled India* (Calcutta: Rupa, 1992), 287.
5. Jawaharlal Nehru, *The Discovery of India* (New York: John Day, 1946), 325. Cf. Scott's own 'To forget strikes me as the quickest way of making the same mistake again' (*MAM* 119).
6. Harveen Sachdeva Mann, review of Spurling's *Paul Scott* in *Modern*

*Fiction Studies*, 37:4 (Winter 1991), 795.

7. Scott's handling of this issue has attracted much attention. On his research, see Richard M. Johnson, '"Sayed's Trial" in Paul Scott's *A Division of the Spoils*: The Interplay of History, Theme and Purpose', *Library Chronicle of the University of Texas*, 38 (1986), 76–91. For the charge that he was 'constrained by his personal concepts of loyalty', see Degi, 'Paul Scott's Indian Army', 54; for the view that in fact he 'got the psychology of the old nationalists right', see Moore, *Paul Scott's Raj*, 169.
8. Scott's deviation from realist assumptions is seen at its clearest here. On novels which 'present themselves as documentary history *and* as artifice', see Alison Lee, *Realism and Power: Postmodern British Fiction* (London: Routledge, 1990), 36; on the narrator who asserts 'the truth of his tale' before disappearing 'from sight into text', see the editor's Introduction to *The Novel Today: Contemporary Writers on Modern Fiction*, ed. Malcolm Bradbury (London: Fontana, 1977), 10–11.

## CHAPTER 5. THE *RAJ QUARTET*: THEMES

1. See Spurling, *Paul Scott*, 319–20.
2. See Jacob Pandian, *The Making of India and Indian Traditions* (Englewood Cliffs, NJ: Prentice-Hall, 1995), 135.
3. Up to now, the most important characters to have carried the problem of cultural identity for Scott have been Eurasian women (especially Dorothy Gower in *The Alien Sky*). See Gorra for a full discussion of Hari as a vehicle for this concern, from the point of view of what defines 'Englishness' (Gorra, *After Empire*, 15–61).
4. Lady Manners's decision to foster her Indian identity must have helped. Still, she is a very positive figure. For early literary treatments of Eurasians, see H. L. Malchow's *Gothic Images of Race in Nineteenth-Century Britain* (Stanford: Stanford University Press, 1996), 200–10; growing sympathy for them is traced in Allen J. Greenberger's *The British Image of India: A Study of the Literature of Imperialism, 1880–1960* (Oxford: Oxford University Press, 1969), 182–6, and best exemplified in John Masters' Eurasian heroine, Victoria Jones, in *Bhowani Junction* (1954).
5. Allen Boyer sees Merrick as the 'personification of the Raj', in his 'Love, Sex and History in *The Raj Quartet*', *Modern Language Quarterly*, 46:1 (March 1985), 73.
6. Said claims that 'overall condemnation of imperialism' arose only when 'native uprisings' could no longer be dealt with (*Culture and Imperialism*, New York: Vintage, 1994, 241).

7. Gorra, *After Empire*, 6.
8. For example, unlike the ICS recruits, they would not usually have gone to university (see Charles Allen, *Plain Tales from the Raj: Images of British India in the Twentieth Century*, New Delhi: Rupa, 1993, 93).
9. These wives have been blamed for the deterioration of relations with the Indians (see Allen, *Plain Tales*, 197), though Scott speaks up for them in his portraits of Lady Manners, Mabel Layton and Lucy Smalley; for his final word on their 'vital contribution', see Moore, *Paul Scott's Raj*, 158.
10. Boyer, 'Love, Sex and History', 64.
11. Spurling, *Paul Scott*, 306.
12. See Boyer, 'Love, Sex and History', 73.
13. See Spurling, *Paul Scott*, 341–3. Spurling notes the similarities with the way Hari is treated by Merrick, but not the contrast between the two victims' responses.
14. Tim Piggot-Smith, the actor who took the role of Merrick in the television adaptation, has testified to this – in the end, he told Debbie Thrower in a BBC Radio 2 interview on 15 August 1997, 'I couldn't understand why people thought he was bad'.
15. Scott found Mrs Moore deeply significant (*MAM* 125); for discussions of Forster and Scott, see especially Ralph J. Crane's *Inventing India: A History of India in English-Language Fiction* (London: Macmillan, 1992), 122–4; and Benita Parry's 'Paul Scott's Raj', *South Asian Review*, 8:4 (July–October 1974), 369. Both mention the connection between Mrs Moore and Lady Manners, without however noting the latter's more practical side.
16. See Francine S. Weinbaum, *Paul Scott: A Critical Study* (Austin: University of Texas Press, 1992), 101–2. Weinbaum misses the positive implications which I discuss here, implications borne out by Scott's own later projections for the characters (see Moore, *Paul Scott's Raj*, 203–4).
17. A moving account of the hopeful ending of Philoctetes's story can be found in Seamus Heaney's *The Cure at Troy* (London: Faber, 1990).
18. Cheetahs are known as hunting leopards, and leopards belong to the panther family. NB, leopards are also associated with treachery in *The Corrida at San Feliu*. Wilde (whose work, like T. E. Lawrence's, Scott had long admired) used panthers specifically to refer to homosexuality, describing his dinners with Lord Arthur Douglas and assorted rent boys as 'feasting with panthers' (quoted in Sheridan Morley, *Oscar Wilde*, London: Weidenfeld and Nicolson, 1976, 90).
19. A. Parthasarathy, *The Symbolism of Hindu Gods and Rituals*, 4th ed. (Bombay: Vedanta Life, 1984), 30.

## CHAPTER 6. *STAYING ON*, AND AFTERWARDS

1. There are several examples of this in the *Raj Quartet* itself, where Pankot is the name of the place where William Conway spends some of his early boyhood in *The Birds of Paradise*, and the Resident of Gopalakand who 'isn't... in the least helpful' to the Nawab of Mirat is none other than William's uncompromising father, Sir Robert Conway (*DSp* 548).
2. See Spurling, *Paul Scott*, 410–13.
3. Rao, *Paul Scott*, 146.
4. Weinbaum, *Paul Scott*, 191.
5. Mollie M. Mahood, 'Paul Scott's Guardians', *The Yearbook of English Studies*, 13 (1983), 244.
6. See Steven Connor's useful comments on postwar novel sequences, *The English Novel in History, 1950–1995* (London: Routledge, 1996), 136–9.
7. *Clea* (London: Faber, 1963), 116. There is much in Pursewarden's notebook about the narrative 'four-card trick' which might be applied to the *Raj Quartet*.
8. Gorra, *Paul Scott*, 29.
9. Iris Murdoch, 'Against Dryness: A Polemical Sketch', in *The Novel Today: Contemporary Writers on Modern Fiction*, ed. Malcolm Bradbury (London: Fontana, 1977), 30.
10. Patrick Swinden, *Paul Scott: Images of India* (London: Macmillan, 1980), 1.
11. Weinbaum, *Paul Scott*, 157. Even Weinbaum's more positive and helpful concluding chapter foregrounds what she sees as Scott's 'mourning of an integrated self' (p. 204).
12. Lodge, *Working with Structuralism*, 15.

# Select Bibliography

(The place of publication is London, unless otherwise stated; where possible, British Library shelfmarks are given for books which proved hard to find elsewhere.)

## WORKS BY PAUL SCOTT

*I, Gerontius – A Trilogy: 'The Creation' – 'The Dream' – 'The Cross'*, Resurgam Younger Poets Series, No. 5. (Favil Press, 1940). BL shelfmark: 11613.d.3/5.

*Pillars of Salt*, in *Four Jewish Plays*, ed. Harold Rubinstein (London and Southampton: Camelot Press, Victor Gollancz, 1948). BL shelfmark: 11783.aaa.102.

*Johnnie Sahib* (Eyre and Spottiswoode, 1952; repr. Heinemann, 1968; St Albans: Panther, 1979).

*The Alien Sky* (Eyre and Spottiswoode, 1953; repr. Heinemann, 1967; St Albans: Panther, 1975; US edn., *Six Days in Marapore*, New York: Doubleday, 1953).

*A Male Child* (Eyre and Spottiswoode, 1956; repr. Heinemann, 1956; new edn. 1968; St Albans: Panther, 1974; US edn. New York: Dutton, 1957).

*The Mark of the Warrior* (Eyre and Spottiswoode, 1958; repr. Heinemann, 1967; St Albans: Panther, 1979).

*The Chinese Love Pavilion* (Eyre and Spottiswoode, 1960; repr. Mayflower, 1967; St Albans: Panther, 1973; US edn., *The Love Pavilion*, New York: William Morrow, 1960).

*The Birds of Paradise* (Eyre and Spottiswoode, 1962; repr. Penguin, 1964; St Albans: Panther, 1975; US edn. New York: William Morrow, 1962).

*The Bender: Pictures from an Exhibition of Middle Class Portraits* (Secker and Warburg, 1963; repr. Penguin, 1964; St Albans: Panther, 1965; US edn., *The Bender*, New York: William Morrow, 1963).

*The Corrida at San Feliu* (Secker and Warburg, 1964; repr. St Albans: Panther, 1974; US edn. New York: William Morrow, 1964).

*The Jewel in the Crown* (Heinemann, 1966; repr. St Albans: Panther, 1973; Mandarin, 1996; US edn. New York: William Morrow, 1966).
*The Day of the Scorpion* (Heinemann, 1968; repr. St Albans: Panther, 1970; Mandarin, 1996; US edn. New York: William Morrow, 1968).
*The Towers of Silence* (Heinemann, 1971; repr. St Albans: Panther, 1973; Mandarin, 1996; US edn. New York: William Morrow, 1972).
*A Division of the Spoils* (Heinemann, 1975; repr. St Albans: Panther, 1977; Mandarin, 1996; US edn. New York: William Morrow, 1975).
*The Raj Quartet* (one-volume edition), (Heinemann, 1976; US edn. New York: William Morrow, 1976).
*Staying On* (Heinemann, 1977; repr. Mandarin, 1996; US edn. New York: William Morrow, 1976).
*After the Funeral*, illus. Sally Scott (Andoversford: Whittington Press and Heinemann, 1979). BL shelfmark: Cup.510.dga.21.
*My Appointment with the Muse: Essays, 1961–75*, ed. Shelley C. Reece (Heinemann, 1986; US edn., *On Writing and the Novel*, New York: Morrow, 1987).

## Miscellaneous writings

'Death of a Hero' and 'Time' (sonnets), in *Poems of This War*, ed. Patricia Ledward and Colin Strang (Cambridge University Press, 1942).
*Lines of Communication* (radio play, 1953), manuscript in the Harry Ransom Humanities Research Center, University of Texas, Austin.
*Sahibs and Memsahibs* (radio play, 1955), manuscript in the Harry Ransom Humanities Research Center, University of Texas, Austin.

NOTE. Some of Scott's book reviews for the *Times Literary Supplement* and *Country Life* are listed by K. B. Rao and F. S. Weinbaum (see below); most of Scott's manuscripts are held at the Harry Ransom Humanities Research Center; other material is held at the McFarlin Library, University of Tulsa, Oklahoma.

## BIOGRAPHICAL AND CRITICAL STUDIES

Banerjee, Jacqueline, 'A Living Legacy: An Indian View of Paul Scott's India', *London Magazine*, 20 (April/May 1980), 97–104.
Beloff, Max, 'The End of the Raj: Paul Scott's Novels as History, *Encounter*, 272 (May 1976), 65–70.
Boyer, Allen, 'Love, Sex, and History in *The Raj Quartet*', *Modern Language Quarterly*, 46 (March 1985), 64–80. Argues that Scott uses Merrick's homosexuality to show the causes of the failure of the imperial relationship.
Brandt, George W., '*The Jewel in the Crown* (Paul Scott – Ken Taylor). The

Literary Serial; or The Art of Adaptation', in Brandt (ed.), *British Television Drama in the 1980s* (Cambridge: Cambridge University Press, 1993), 196–213.

Colwell, Danny, '"I am your Mother and your Father": Paul Scott's *Raj Quartet* and the Dissolution of Imperial Identity', in Bart Moore-Gilbert (ed.), *Writing India, 1757–1990* (Manchester: Manchester University Press, 1996). Situates Scott on ambiguous middle ground between the colonial and the postcolonial; supports a postmodern reading of the *Quartet*.

Crane, Ralph J., *Inventing India: A History of India in English-Language Fiction* (London: Macmillan, 1992). Helpful sections on the *Raj Quartet* and *Staying On*.

Degi, Bruce J., 'Paul Scott's Indian National Army: *The Mark of the Warrior* and *The Raj Quartet*', CLIO: *A Journal of Literature, History, and the Philosophy of History*, 18 (Fall 1988), 41–54.

Gorra, Michael, *After Empire: Scott, Naipaul, Rushdie* (Chicago: Chicago University Press, 1997).

Hannah, Donald, '"Dirty Typescripts and Very Dirty Typescripts": Paul Scott's Working Methods in *The Raj Quartet*', *Journal of Commonwealth Literature*, 27:1 (1992), 149–70. Draws usefully on unpublished manuscripts to bring out the experience of 're-enactment' shared by author, characters and reader (p. 166).

Johnson, Richard M., '"Sayed's Trial" in Paul Scott's *A Division of the Spoils*: The Interplay of History, Theme, and Purpose', *Library Chronicle of the University of Texas*, 38 (1986), 76–91. Claims this episode rings false on the personal level, but praises Scott's handling of the historical issues.

Mahood, Mollie, M., 'Paul Scott's Guardians', *The Yearbook of English Studies*, 13 (1983), 244–58. Emphasizes Scott's 'positive values' (p. 246); especially good on the female characters of the *Quartet*.

Mann, Harveen Sachdeva, review of Spurling's *Paul Scott* in *Modern Fiction Studies*, 37 (Winter 1991), 794–6.

Mellors, John, 'Raj Mahal: Paul Scott's India Quartet', *London Magazine*, 15 (June/July 1975), 62–7.

Moore, Robin, *Paul Scott's Raj* (Heinemann, 1990). Sympathetic approach from a well-informed historical perspective. Makes full use of unpublished materials.

Muggeridge, Malcolm, 'Eastern Settings, Western Writers', review of *Staying On* in *New York Times Book Review*, 21 August 1977, pp. 1, 36.

Parry, Benita, 'Paul Scott's Raj', *South Asian Review*, 8 (July–October 1975), 359–69. Finds ambiguities in Scott's attitudes.

Rao, K. Bhaskara, *Paul Scott* (Boston: Twayne, 1980). Good for basic information about the Indian background.

Rubin, David, *After the Raj: British Novels of India since 1947* (Hanover: University Press of New England, 1986).

Rushdie, Salman, 'Outside the Whale', *American Film*, 10 (January 1985), 16, 70, 72–3. Vituperative general comments; largely concerned with screen versions of the Raj.

Scanlan, Margaret, 'The Disappearance of History: Paul Scott's *Raj Quartet*', CLIO: *A Journal of Literature, History, and the Philosophy of History*, 15 (Winter 1986), 153–69. Emphasizes Scott's pessimism.

Spurling, Hilary, *Paul Scott: A Life* (Pimlico, 1991). The only biography, and likely to remain so. Indispensable.

Swinden, Patrick, *Paul Scott*, Writers and Their Work Series (Windsor: Profile, 1982). Still a useful introductory essay.

——, *Paul Scott: Images of India* (Macmillan, 1980). An enquiry into 'the position of India as a country and an idea in [Scott's] mind' (p. 4).

Tedesco, Janis, 'Staying On: The Final Connection', *Western Humanities Review*, 39:3 (Autumn 1985), 195–211. Good on links and parallels with the *Quartet*.

——, and Janet Popham, *An Introduction to the Raj Quartet* (Lanham, Maryland: University Press of America, 1985). Helpful for tracing particular motifs or inter-relations through the novels. Works entirely within the text (no critical debate, no bibliography).

Weinbaum, Francine S., *Paul Scott: A Critical Study* (Austin: University of Texas Press, 1992). The most detailed critical study, with an emphasis on Scott's fragmented personality and desire for unity.

Williamson, Karina, review of Rao's *Paul Scott* and Swinden's *Paul Scott: Images of India*, *Notes and Queries*, 30:3 (June 1983), 267–8.

Zorn, Jean G., 'Talk with Paul Scott', *New York Times Book Review*, 21 August 1977, 37.

## BACKGROUND READING

Allen, Charles, *Plain Tales from the Raj: Images of British India in the Twentieth Century* (New Delhi: Rupa, 1993). Essential social history of the Raj, also published by André Deutsch and the BBC, 1975.

—— *Raj: A Scrapbook of British India, 1877–1947* (André Deutsch, 1977).

Barr, Pat, *The Memsahibs: The Women of Victorian India* (Century, 1989). Sympathetic study of some earlier 'mems' – good background for such characters as Lady Manners; moving account of the 1857 Bibighar massacre.

Bradbury, Malcolm, Introduction to *The Novel Today: Contemporary Writers on Modern Fiction*, ed. Malcolm Bradbury (Fontana, 1977).

Connor, Steven, *The English Novel in History, 1950–1995* (Routledge, 1996).

Diver, Maud, *The Englishwoman in India* (Blackwood, 1909).

Durrell, Lawrence, *Clea* (Faber, 1963). Interesting comments on the 'four- or five-decker' narrative sequence (p. 117).

Fasteau, Marc Feigin, *The Male Machine* (New York: McGraw-Hill, 1974).

Greenberger, Allen J., *The British Image of India: A Study of the Literature of Imperialism, 1880–1960* (Oxford University Press, 1969). The Epilogue on the later period provides a context for Scott, though his own work during this time has been overlooked.

Gutteridge, Bernard, *Traveller's Eye* (Routledge, 1947). Wartime poetry about experiences in India and Burma.

Hubel, Teresa, *Whose India? The Independence Struggle in British and Indian Fiction and History* (Leicester University Press, 1996). Useful background in chapter 6, 'Nostalgia and 1947'.

Jourard, Sidney M., 'Some Lethal Aspects of the Male Role', in Joseph H. Pleck and Jack Sawyer (eds.), *Men and Masculinity* (Englewood Cliffs, NJ: Prentice-Hall, 1974).

Kulke, Hermann, and Dietmar Rothermund, *A History of India* (Routledge, 1990). Excellent chapters (6 and 7) on the colonial period and the freedom movement.

Lazarus, Neil, *Resistance in Postcolonial African Fiction* (New Haven: Yale University Press, 1990).

Lee, Alison, *Realism and Power; Postmodern British Fiction* (Routledge, 1990). Chapter 2 considers the postmodernist challenge to traditional concepts of history.

Lewis, Alun, *Selected Poems*, ed. Jeremy Hooker and Gweno Lewis (Unwin, 1981). See especially 'The Jungle'.

——— *In the Green Tree* (Allen and Unwin, 1948). Letters and short stories about army experiences in India and Burma during the war.

Lodge, David, *Working with Structuralism: Essays and Reviews on Nineteenth- and Twentieth-Century Literature* (Ark Paperbacks, 1986). Brief but lucid classification of postmodernist techniques (pp. 12–16).

MacMillan, Margaret, *Women of the Raj* (Thames and Hudson, 1996). See chapter 6, 'Women in Danger'.

Majumdar, R. C., H. C. Raychaudhuri and Kalikinkar Datta, *An Advanced History of India*, 4th edn. (Madras, Bombay, Calcutta, Delhi: Macmillan India, 1978). Many times reprinted, standard higher-level Indian textbook.

Malchow, H. L., *Gothic Images of Race in Nineteenth-Century Britain* (Stanford: Stanford University Press, 1996). Useful section on India, pp. 200–210.

Mason, Philip, *The Men Who Ruled India* (Calcutta, Allahbad, Bombay, New Delhi: Rupa, 1992). Sensitive and balanced account.

Masters, John, *Bhowani Junction* (Penguin, 1960). Interesting for the character of Colonel Rodney Savage – a 'leopard' who improves on acquaintance (p. 46) – as well as for the treatment of Eurasians.

Morahan, Christopher, 'All the Raj', letter to the *Listener*, 29 March 1984.

Morley, Sheridan, *Oscar Wilde* (Weidenfeld and Nicolson, 1976).

Mosley, Leonard, *The Last Days of the British Raj* (New York: Harcourt, Brace, and World, 1961).

Mosse, George L., *The Image of Man: The Creation of Modern Masculinity* (Oxford University Press, 1996).

Murdoch, Iris, 'Against Dryness: A Polemical Sketch', in Malcolm Bradbury (ed.), *The Novel Today: Contemporary Writers on Modern Fiction* (Fontana, 1977).

Nehru, Jawaharal, *The Discovery of India* (New York: John Day, 1946).

Pandian, Jacob, *The Making of India and Indian Traditions* (Englewood Cliffs, NJ: Prentice-Hall, 1995).

Parry, Benita, *Delusions and Discoveries: Studies on India in the British Imagination, 1880–1930* (New Delhi: Orient Longman/Allen Lane, 1974).

Parthasarathy, A., *The Symbolism of Hindu Gods and Rituals*, 4th edn. (Bombay: Vedanta Life Institute, 1994).

Piggott-Smith, Tim, *Out of India* (Duckworth, 2nd edn., 1977).

Said, Edward, W., *Culture and Imperialism* (New York: Vintage, 1994).

Sarup, Madan, *Jacques Lacan* (Harvester Wheatsheaf, 1992).

Savarkar, Vinayak Damodar, *The Indian War of Independence* (Bombay: Phoenix Publications, 1947). The other side of the picture – inflammatory; unfortunately, withdrawn from publication in England.

Taylor, P. J. O., *A Star Shall Fall: India 1857* (New Delhi: Indus–HarperCollins imprint, 1993). Detailed account of the Bibighar massacre by an old India hand who still has a weekly column in the Delhi *Statesman*. BL shelfmark: YA.1993.1.21254.

# Index

# WRITERS AND THEIR WORK

*"... this series promises to outshine its own obviously high reputation."*
**_Times Higher Education Supplement_**

*"... will build into a fine multi-volume critical encyclopaedia of English literature."*
**_Library Review & Reference Review_**

*"... Excellent, informative, readable, and recommended."*
**_NATE News_**

*"written by outstanding contemporary critics, whose expertise is flavoured by unashamed enthusiasm for their subjects and the series' diverse aspirations."*
**_Times Educational Supplement_**

*"A useful and timely addition to the ranks of the lit crit and reviews genre. Written in an accessible and authoritative style."*
**_Library Association Record_**

## WRITERS AND THEIR WORK

| Title | Author |
|---|---|
| Alfred Tennyson | *Seamus Perry* |
| Anita Desai | *Elaine Yee Lin Ho* |
| Anthony Trollope | *Andrew Sanders* |
| Byron | *Drummond Bone* |
| C.S. Lewis | *William Gray* |
| Charles Dickens | *Rod Mengham* |
| Chinua Achebe | *Nahem Yousaf* |
| D.H. Lawrence | *Linda Ruth Williams* |
| E.M. Forster | *Nicholas Royle* |
| Franz Kafka | *Michael Wood* |
| George Eliot | *Josephine McDonagh* |
| George Orwell | *Douglas Kerr* |
| Gerard Manley Hopkins | *Daniel Brown* |
| Harold Pinter | *Mark Taylor-Batty* |
| Henrik Ibsen, 2nd edition | *Sally Ledger* |
| Henry James—The Later Writing | *Barbara Hardy* |
| Jane Austen | *Robert Miles* |
| John Keats | *Kelvin Everest* |
| Joseph Conrad | *Cedric Watts* |
| Leo Tolstoy | *John Bayley* |
| Oscar Wilde | *Alexandra Warwick* |
| Paul Scott | *Jacqueline Banerjee* |
| Percy Bysshe Shelley | *Paul Hamilton* |
| Philip Larkin, 2nd Edition | *Laurence Lerner* |
| Robert Browning | *John Woolford* |
| Rudyard Kipling | *Jan Montefiore* |
| Samuel Beckett | *Sinéad Mooney* |

## WRITERS AND THEIR WORK

| Title | Author |
|---|---|
| Samuel Taylor Coleridge | *Stephen Bygrave* |
| Shashi Deshpande | *Amrita Bhalla* |
| Sir Walter Scott | *Harriet Harvey Wood* |
| Stephen Crane | *Kevin J. Hayes* |
| Swinburne | *Catherine Maxwell* |
| Sylvia Plath, 2nd edition | *Elisabeth Bronfen* |
| T.S. Eliot | *Colin MacCabe* |
| Ted Hughes | *Susan Bassnett* |
| Thomas Hardy, 2nd Edition | *Peter Widdowson* |
| V.S. Naipaul | *Suman Gupta* |
| Victorian Quest Romance | *Robert Fraser* |
| Virginia Woolf, 2nd Edition | *Laura Marcus* |
| W.B. Yeasts | *Edward Larrissy* |
| William Blake | *Steve Vine* |
| William Golding, 2nd Edition | *Kevin McCarron* |
| William Makepeace Thackeray | *Richard Salmon* |
| Wole Soyinka | *Mpalive-Hangson Msiska* |